HOUSING
FOR PEOPLE
OR FOR PROFIT ?
JOHN COWLEY

Illustrations by Paul F. Downton

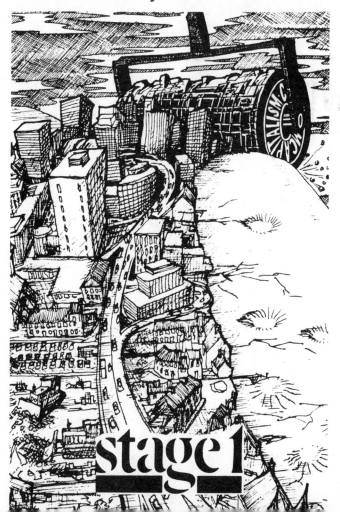

stage 1

Acknowledgements

Many people have helped in the preparation of this book. I am particularly indebted to the members, past and present, of the Camden Square Area Tenants & Residents Association, especially Margaret Bruen and Joe Dawson. At various times when it was needed a number of people gave me special advice and encouragement and I wish to thank them: Ron and Margaret Bailey, Frank Burton, Alec and Evelyn Cowley, Jim Duggan, Adah Kay, Charles Legg, Marjorie Mayo and Sue O'Sullivan.

John Cowley, London, July 1979

For Tom and Dan

British Library Cataloguing in Publication Data
Cowley, John, *b.1939*
    Housing, for people or for profit?
    1. Housing – Great Britain
    I. Title
    301.5′4′0941   HD7333.A3
    ISBN 0–85035–035–2
    ISBN 0–85035–036–0 Pbk

stage 1, 47 Red Lion Street, London, WC1R 4PF

Phototypeset by Input Typesetting Ltd, London SW19
Printed and bound in Great Britain by Whitstable Litho Ltd, Whitstable, Kent

Contents

Introduction

Unfulfilled needs

Housing meets one of the basic needs of human survival. With the historical development of society, the ways and means of socially meeting that need have changed and become increasingly complex. The need itself has grown and today encompasses much more than just protection from the elements. In a rich and developed capitalist society such as Britain, with its emphasis on consumption and home life, housing plays a vital role in daily life. The space a dwelling provides for individual and family life, its state of physical repair and upkeep, and the cost of its use, are issues of enormous concern to people and are constantly manifesting themselves in struggles undertaken by individuals and groups to defend and improve their housing conditions. Capitalism itself, in the fullness of its development, has generated social wants, not only in relation to housing but in other spheres of social experience such as work and sexuality, that it cannot satisfy. Why this is so with housing and its significance for the development of working class politics is the subject matter of this book.

A lot has been written on the question of housing in Britain, particularly in terms of the social history of working class dwellings and the emergence of housing as an object of state intervention and party politics. But few people have tried to explain the nature of housing in a capitalist society and its place in political struggle. The need for such clarification is now a matter of some urgency, as the housing situation is in the process of deteriorating and may well do so quite rapidly during the nineteen eighties. New house building is at an all-time low. There is very little private or local authority building projected for the coming years. The present Government is cutting the funds going into local authority housing, selling off some of the better Council stock, and offering private landlords the possibility of highly profitable short-term lets. An increasing number of individuals and families will find themselves trapped in dwellings falling into disrepair, becoming obsolete and unfit for habitation at a time of little building activity, while the price of accommodation, whether in the form of rent or interest payments, continues to rise. These developments make all the more pressing the proper understanding of why there is a recurring housing problem.

Defining the problem

There are many facets to the housing problem, not the least of which is that it can co-exist with a surplus of dwellings. From the mid-1970s, the first time since the Industrial Revolution, the number of dwellings surpassed the number of families and individuals—households—living or wishing to live in their own home. England and Wales have more than 18 million dwellings, an excess of some half million over the estimated number of households.[1] The extent and significance of the surplus is open to serious questioning—where are the dwellings situated, what is their state of repair and to whom do they belong? What is not in dispute, however, is that the housing stock is larger than it has ever been before and is numerically somewhat greater than the number of people wanting homes. But despite this apparently favourable situation, quite unique in the history of this country, there still exists a housing problem.

In every city and town, the centres of industrial and commercial activity and wealth, people live in damp, poorly insulated and inadequately heated houses, perhaps sharing with another family or individuals a cooker on the landing and a single bathroom. For others it is a matter of living in one room divided in two by hardboard, a gas ring and wash basin next to the bed, a suitcase on the wardrobe, no privacy of sound from the other occupied rooms, and the inconvenience of sharing with the whole house the one toilet which it is no-one's responsibility to clean. Newly formed couples and children grown into adulthood stay with their families, or become homeless and are forced to take temporary local authority accommodation or perhaps risk the trials and tribulations of squatting council-owned housing awaiting demolition or renovation. Hundreds of thousands of people live in conditions which fall far short of what today are the officially recognised minimum standards of residential accommodation. There are about one million dwellings, presently lived in, that are substandard and lack at least one basic amenity such as a bath, indoor flush toilet or hot running water. A further million flats and houses need substantial repairs costing £1,000 or more. In all, millions of people are affected by poor conditions such as these.[2]

To these problems of the actual condition and upkeep of parts of the housing stock must be added those of the insecurity and anxiety experienced daily by individuals and families because their landlord wants vacant possession of the flat, or simply because of the difficulties they have in meeting the weekly rent or mortgage payments. The pressure to move may have many causes: perhaps the main wage-earner in the household has died, or the whole street is to be razed to the ground and redeveloped, or maybe the house is to be gutted and modernised by the owners, be they private or public.

For most of this century, successive governments have expressed confidence in their ability to solve the housing problem. It is seen as being essentially residual in nature, an imbalance arising in a period of economic change and growth. So the existence of a problem in the provision of housing is seen as being due to a number of quite distinct factors, all of which can be solved. The first and most important facing the policy-maker is said to be the unforeseen development such as the massive migration to London and the South-East during the past fifty years. Then there is the unforeseen natural or social disaster, which for this country was World War II, resulting in the destruction of half a million houses and substantial damage to 3½ million more.[3] At the same time there is the elementary problem of a shortage of reliable information on which to base policy decisions, such as the numbers of private households seeking accommodation, their size, changes in the age at which people are marrying,

immigration and movements in employment oppor-
tunities, as well as the actual condition of the housing
stock and the availability of financing and possible
future changes in interest rates.

Bearing in mind these factors of the unforeseen and
the unknown, the solution is seen as lying in the
proper combination of additions and improvements to
the existing stock of dwellings and a skilful manipulation of rent levels and mortgage rates. This has
resulted in successive Governments promoting slum
clearance schemes and new building and modernisation programmes and adjustments to rent and mortgage interest controls. Each Government expresses its
confidence in being able to finally solve the problem.
Following World War I, the Lloyd George Government
proclaimed it would build "Homes fit for Heroes", a
pledge it failed to fulfil. Later, in 1933, the Minister of
Health, Sir Hilton Young, responsible in those days
for housing as well, thought "five years" sufficient to
see the problem solved. A similar view was taken in
1954: "Five years or so" was the estimate of the then
Minister of Housing, Harold Macmillan. In 1971 the
Minister responsible for housing thought it might take
the best part of ten years to get rid of all the slums
and provide the people with decent homes.[4] Later
Ministers, notably Peter Shore and Michael Heseltine,
were equally confident that the housing problem—the
shortages, disrepair, lack of amenities, dangers to
safety and health, overcrowding and the many
unhoused—was capable of solution. They believed
that in their capacity as Ministers with special responsibility for housing they could devise the policy that
would resolve the matter, if not once and for all, then
at least for the time being. All the elements, including
the excess of stock, appeared to be present and ready
to be correctly and skilfully combined to produce the
solution so much needed. But unless it is known why
there is a housing shortage even in the very moment
of plenty, the solution cannot even be constructed in
thought, let alone in reality.

The question

Why is there a problem? How can there be more dwellings than households and yet a shortage? And why, when the elements of a solution appear to be there, does the problem grow? The answer lies in the fact that although housing in its distribution appears to consist of a myriad of individual private and public tenancies and owner-occupiers, in reality the greater part of the housing stock is in very few hands. Many of the houses in owner-occupation effectively belong to financial institutions specialising in investing in housing—the building societies. The other major tenure today, the public sector, is also deeply indebted to and dependent upon private financing. In reality, underlying the legal forms of occupancy rights are the actual financial arrangements which give effective command over the greater part of the housing stock to the institutions of private finance. The explanation for this concentration of ownership lies in the way in which production is socially organised upon the basis of a workforce "exclusively dependent upon wages".[5] Such workers are generally in no position to purchase outright a commodity as expensive as housing, so possession of the housing stock is restricted to a small segment of society.

It is this reality of class ownership which explains the puzzle at the heart of the housing question. Why, after more than a century of genuine progress in the physical construction and standards of dwellings and the destruction of some of the worst slums ever produced by an industrial society, is there ever-present the problem of bad housing conditions and dwellings unfit for habitation? Once again the answer lies in the class character of property relations which ensure that, despite the extraordinary expansion in production and the wealth of society as a whole, the inequalities in its distribution remain. This is as true for housing as it is for the distribution of wealth and income generally. Progress, therefore, is relative and must be judged in the light of the totality of the wealth produced by society.

"A house may be large or small; as long as the surrounding houses are equally small it satisfies all social
demands for a dwelling. But if a palace arises beside
the little house, the little house shrinks into a hut. The
little house shows now that its owner has only very
slight or no demands to make: and however high it
may shoot up in the course of civilisation, if the neighbouring palace grows to an equal or even greater
extent, the dweller in the relatively small house will
feel more and more uncomfortable, dissatisfied and
cramped within its four walls."[6]

Capitalism has generated social wants for a standard
of living and a quality of life that it can not satisfy. The
mass of people may not be starving, but they have
wants concerning their individual and social life, at
work and at home, that go beyond the pay check.

Beyond capitalist solutions

The housing problem is rooted in the very structure
of the society. Any movement for reform amongst
tenants, the homeless, or any other housing interest
group, in challenging the effects of the present system,
continually faces the limits of such reforms. But if the
various elements of the tenants movement—which
may include not only council and private tenants, but
people with other forms of tenures too, including
some lease-holders and owner-occupiers, and also
homeless people—are to challenge the roots of their
problems and dis-satisfactions, they will have to play
their part in advancing anti-capitalist politics within
the workers movement generally. This will involve
recognizing that municipalisation is not the same thing
as socialism, but is a partial solution to working class
housing needs achievable under capitalism. Just as the
nationalisation of mining or the railways, although an
advance for the workers in these industries, represents
not socialism in embryo but the intervention of the
capitalist state, similarly with council housing: it is a
reform of capitalism in response to the demands of
the working class. If the movement around housing
issues is not to be easily co-opted into the apparatus
of the state, it needs to be informed by a conception

of what will be a fundamental and lasting solution to the housing question. This will require a complete rupture with any of the forms of ownership that exist today on the basis of private finance and will require the application of the principle of social ownership and popular control to the entire housing stock and its provision and allocation.

It is hoped that this study of housing in a capitalist society will be of use to all interested, or directly involved, in housing struggles and wanting to advance their level of organization and politics. The analysis should also be helpful to those active in related struggles in other spheres such as health, education, transport and the environment who are looking for connections and links. In practice such links will be fragile so long as the backbone of the workers movement, the trade unions, and the political left generally fail to grasp the real importance of these potentially anti-capitalist movements that are erupting with ever greater frequency outside the workplace. Housing is just one such area of struggle where the long-run political stability of capitalism is at stake and vulnerable.

Chapter 1
Capital and the housing stock

Capital

It is fairly simple to conjure up a picture of the housing stock: all those houses and flats, mansions and cottages at present standing and capable of being lived in. Capital, however, is not so easy, for it refers not to a tangible thing such as a house or even a piece of machinery, but to a relationship. Engels defines capital as "the command over the unpaid labour of others".[1] We live in a society in which the immediate producers, particularly those engaged in farming, mining, manufacture and transport, are paid a wage. The wage is not payment for a person's labour, for the amount of work done in a day, but is the purchase price for the individual's ability to work. Wages cover the costs of producing and maintaining that ability as embodied in the class of immediate producers. This means covering the costs of food, clothing, shelter and relaxation. That is what wages are for. Capital is command over the unpaid labour, the surplus produced over and above these necessary costs of the immediate producers. It is precisely this "command over unpaid labour"—capital, in its relationship to paid labour, the wage worker—which is at the heart of the social organisation and historical development of capitalist society.

To understand the present composition and use of the housing stock we need to examine its history: how it came into existence, when, where, and why. That history is inseparable from the dynamic of the capital/wage-labour relation. In terms of this country there are three important phases in the history of the housing stock. First came the early phase of industrial development, the industrial revolution, and the first modern towns: the hell-holes of factories and homes in which the industrial proletariat was born. This covers the period from the 1780s through to the 1840s, in which the main centres of urban living were established in this country. Then came the imperial age from the 1850s to the 1930s, in which the rentier petit bourgeoisie, the private landlord, dominated the housing stock in terms of its ownership and construction. Finally, the period from the 1930s to the present saw the concentration of capital into a very few hands—monopoly capital—and housing becoming dominated by a complex of financial institutions—lenders of money.

Industry and town

The period covering the last decades of the 18th century through to the middle of the 19th century was one of remarkable industrial development. The transformation of production into the mills, foundries and workshops of the industrial revolution brought about a rapid and, for the most part, unplanned growth of towns. Villages were engulfed by the rapid spread of manufacturing centres and the quick erection of cheap and usually insanitary housing, having no piped water and poor or non-existent drainage, built especially for the new factory hands. In the more rural areas the factory, mine or mill owner often built the housing. Edward Ackroyd and Titus Salt were among the more enlightened and paternalistic builders of company towns. The latter commanded as well as "his 'steady, well disposed and well beloved work people', a return on capital of 4% on his workers' housing".[2] At the time it was, as Engels said, "a necessary part of the total investment of capital, and a very profitable one, both directly and indirectly".[3] It gave the capitalist both a source of income and greater control over his workforce: out of work, out of home. Many of these factory villages grew quickly into towns.

Where the population was already in fairly large concentrations, as in Manchester and some of the port towns such as Liverpool and Bristol, and, of course, London (which as early as 1750 comprised one-tenth of the population), housing for the workers was provided either by small private speculative ventures or from an already existing housing stock rented out by the room for workers and their families. The concentration and development of large-scale industry, with its inter-connecting requirements of materials, power and labour, brought about the growth of a number of large urban centres in the early decades of the 19th century. In addition to London, there was the Greater Manchester area, the West Midlands, West Yorkshire, Merseyside and Tyneside.

By the middle of the century the characteristic pattern of urban settlement was well established: an inner commercial, administrative centre of shops, offices, public buildings and warehouses, slowly declining in population, surrounded by working class districts in which homes and workshops were generally in close proximity. The middle classes tended to live in the more spacious outer suburbs, and the upper classes lived still further out in their villas surrounded by extensive gardens, on higher land away from the noise and the smoke, where they could partake of "the pure breath of heaven".[4]

This early phase of industrial and urban development was accomplished with little overall direction or regulation. The principal source of new housing stock specifically for working class use was industrial capital itself. On the one hand, numerous factory owners and, on the other, a mass of individual builders erected cheap housing close to new places of work. In these decades men, women and children were often working twelve hours a day, six days a week, and needed to be within walking distance of their place of work. The housing was generally crowded together in narrow, unpaved and ill-lit streets. By the third and fourth decades of the century, back-to-back houses were common to most towns. "In 1840 between 7,000 and 8,000 of Nottingham's 11,000 houses were reported to be back-to-back."[5] Engels described the Old Town of Manchester where every possible space for building was used and "not an inch of space remains between the houses" leaving "passages so narrow that two people cannot pass". The houses were "packed together in disorderly confusion in impudent defiance of all reasonable principles of town planning".[6] The housing itself was in poor condition and insanitary, and families were confined to one or two rooms, sharing an outside lavatory and water pump. Home for the masses was a source of ill-health, much misery and early death.

Investing capital directly into the construction of workplace and dwellings was characteristic of the early decades of rapid urban growth. But by the 1850s labour was becoming less scarce and the element of paternalism in capital's relation to labour was waning, so the need and interest in such investment came to an end. There were exceptions. The idea that industry had created the appalling slums inhabited by the workers filled some industrialists with a sense of guilt. Bourneville and Port Sunlight were two company-owned garden villages built towards the close of the century. William Hesketh Lever, the first Viscount Leverhulme, disliked the unions and wished to improve the motivation and discipline of his workforce. In 1889 he started Port Sunlight on the Merseyside, building cottages and houses in mock tudor style to house the employees of his soap business. Grandiose in conception, they remained isolated schemes. They were not copied by other industrialists, as the necessity for such was past.[7]

The legacy of such investment, the employer as landlord, survives to this day; coal-mining and farming are the two main cases. Almost one in four miners still live in dwellings owned by the National Coal Board.[8] Much of this housing stems from the early decades of the 19th century, and, as well as being below present day standards, also suffers from years of neglect. The one area in which housing is still taken as "a necessary part of the total investment of capital" is farming. Here, the need to be close to work because of the importance of weather conditions, coupled with the farmer's desire to maintain, against the pull of the towns, a captive and low paid labour force, combined to preserve down to the present this unity of employer and landlord.[9] Only with the passing of the Rent (Agriculture) Act in 1976 have farm workers gained protected tenancies equivalent to other private tenants.[10]

The rentier petit bourgeoisie

The second phase in the life of the housing stock runs from mid-Victorian times through to the great crisis of the 1930s, the period of mass unemployment and breakdown in capitalist production. These phases are not separated by clear borderlines, but in each a particular form of capital investment and ownership dominates. In this second period it was the rentier petit bourgeoisie, the small propertied middle class with funds to invest, who came to dominate housing, particularly for the masses. It was the age of fully developed small-scale competitive capitalism. Britain was the leading capitalist power in the world and for a historical moment it straddled the globe. The Empire not only provided new sources for capital investment, particularly the railways, but also increased the income of the middle and upper classes. For the Victorians there was no sounder investment than property itself, in the tangible form of land and buildings. Housing attracted the savings of the petit bourgeoisie—shopkeepers, traders, builders, members of the independent professions of architects and lawyers, and politicians—either directly as landlords or indirectly through channelling their savings into building societies.

The second half of the 19th century was one of continuing expansion of the towns at the expense of the countryside in terms of space and populace. During the 19th century the population as a whole increased more than threefold: from 9 million in 1801 to 32.1 million in 1901. It was in the towns that this growing mass resided. By 1901, 41% of the population of England and Wales lived in the large sprawling urban areas such as Greater London and the Greater Manchester area. A further 21.6% of the population lived in towns of between 50,000 and 200,000 inhabitants.[11] Capitalist development of large-scale industry brought the overwhelming majority of the population into the towns.

Much of the land swallowed up in urban developments was owned by the nobility and by the Crown and the Church. Sometimes the owner developed the land, but more often it was leased or sold in plots to individual builders for development. In London there were the estates of the Duke of Westminster in Grosvenor, the Duke of Bedford in Bloomsbury, the Earl of Cadogan in Chelsea, and the Marquis of Camden in and around Camden Town and Agar Town. The Church and Crown were amongst London's largest private residential landowners. Outside London, the Duke of Hamilton's estate in Lanarkshire included industrial towns, the Duke of Norfolk owned a large part of Sheffield and the Seftons and the Derbys had substantial holdings in the industrial Midlands.[12] Often at this time the landowner divided the land into small plots for development, selling them off at a few shillings per square yard to small builders. Astute or lucky dealings could make a small fortune for those with the savings to invest.

A mass of individuals with small savings were involved in these developments. Sometimes they acted in partnership with the landowner, but more often the actual construction of dwellings seems to have been financed by money borrowed from other private individuals or acquired in the form of a building society mortgage or bank loan. These individuals, members of the petit bourgeoisie, perhaps themselves builders, brought together "the owners of land, the lenders of money, the builders of houses and tenants who needed a home. . . ." They were the private landlord class in the making. They "borrowed the money required to initiate and sustain the whole operation, commissioned the building of houses, managed the property and collected the rents—or formed the essential intermediary linking others who did. . . ." The main contribution of these "landlords" was "to bring the parties to the transaction together, to bear most of the risks involved, and hence to make most of the profits or losses."[13] An illustration of this was the loan made in 1900 by the North Shields Permanent Building Society of £2,964.18s.11d. to the builder, Mr. Sawyer, who purchased land from a local developer, Mrs. Sarah Leitch, widow of the former town clerk of

Tynemouth. On completion, such builders either sold off to private landlords, again almost always financed by a mortgage on the same pattern, or retained houses and acted as landlord themselves.[14] The whole enterprise was small in scale but had the chance of gaining large speculative profits. In London at the peak of the Victorian building boom (1878–1880), Camberwell contained 416 firms or individual builders building 5,670 houses, nearly all speculatively.[15]

In this period of Victorian achievement, some of the worst slums of the earlier decades of the century were pulled down. The cellar dwellings originally built for storage in Liverpool and Manchester were demolished, as were the notorious rookeries, crowded tenements, of Clare Market and St. Giles in central London. Much of the slum clearance was fortuitous: the result of new roads and railways. Nevertheless, the new, wide thoroughfares replacing the old narrow alleyways were seen by contemporaries as a step forward, whereas for the inhabitants it meant much suffering and eventual eviction: "New Oxford Street displaced some 5,000 people, Farringdon Street 40,000, and the construction of Holborn Viaduct, the Embankment, the Law Courts, the enlargement of Smithfield, and the docks (completed in the main in mid-century) all added to the pressure upon housing in the neighbouring districts."[16] The railways had a similar impact. Great areas of housing were torn down to make way for the track and marshalling yards and stations. The railway companies became major owners of inner city land. Typical was Liverpool where 9% of "the central zone" was owned by the railway company by the close of the century.[17] The new railway stations, in their size and grandeur, were monuments to the Victorian faith in capital. St. Pancras Station, along with the track and sidings erected by the Midlands Railway Company, devastated Somers Town, a densely populated working class district of London. Appalling though the slums were, the workers of the area resisted, organising themselves into the Somers Town Defence League. But between 1866 and the late 1870s, 20,000 people were evicted without compensation and in most cases without rehousing.[18]

The consequence of so much of the clearance of these slum areas was that the inhabitants, as Engels noted in the case of Manchester, were for the most part merely displaced into neighbouring streets. He wrote: "This is . . . how the bourgeoisie settles the housing question in practice. The breeding places of disease, the infamous holes and cellars in which the capitalist mode of production confines our workers night after night, are not abolished: they are merely *shifted elsewhere.*"[19]

The housing stock changed throughout the Victorian period. The new housing for the middle and upper classes was spacious, with quarters for the servants, individual gardens and lime trees to preserve privacy. Housing for the working class was built in narrow terraces, back-to-back, with tiny backyards containing the privy. Over half the housing stock in existence on the eve of World War I was built during the preceding 40 years.[20] The growth and concentration of industry both furthered the expansion of towns and at the same time redefined the districts inhabited by the working class and the middle classes. New, cheap forms of mass transport, the railways and trams, extended the distances people could travel to and from work and made possible the growth of suburbs. Deeply involved in the changes in the housing stock, especially the dwellings of the workers, were those with small savings to invest, the petit bourgeoisie. This was the golden age of the private landlord.

Before World War I very few houses were publicly owned. Liverpool, which had some of the worst slums of the late 19th century, was an exception and the local authority had built houses for rent as early as 1869. However, at the outbreak of War in 1914 less than 2% of the housing stock was in local authority possession. Neither was much of the housing stock owned by its occupants: fewer than 1 in 10 families owned their own houses. Before the War a newly built, small two-up, two-down, house cost about £300 to buy, placing it outside the reach of most workers except for a few better-off skilled craftsmen. The overwhelming majority of working class families, including white collar workers and a good proportion of the middle classes, rented their house or their share of a house or room from a private landlord.

The landlord-tenant relationship was not a simple one. Many tenants were in fact sub-tenants of others who in turn were tenants of the whole house and yet known as the "landlady" or "landlord", while the real landlord lived elsewhere. The actual owner and renter of the property also presented a complex picture. In addition to the mass of small landlords owning one or a few houses or a tenement block, there were small property companies owning tens and occasionally hundreds of dwellings. Then there were the charitable trusts, such as the Peabody Trust in London, formed in 1862, owning whole tenement blocks as well as individual houses. The Church and Crown as well as being amongst the largest land-owners in the realm were substantial landlords in their own right.

Before World War I rents were regulated by the open market. There was no form of rent control. In the newer and better housing in working class districts of South Shields and Newcastle, for instance, rents in the first decade of the century ranged from around 2/6 for a one room tenement to 7/- per week for a four bedroom flat. Only the better off workers could afford such rents. For at "this time a skilled fitter on Tyneside earned 35/- a week, a bricklayer 39/7d in summer, a builder's labourer 23/- to 26/-, a shipyard labourer 22/-, a seaman earned 30/-, and dockers earned 5/- a day." The labourers and poorer workers inhabited the slums of the "Old Town", close to the waste-filled river's edge.[21]

The picture presented by South Shields and Newcastle at this time was similar to that which existed nationally.[22] The free determination of rents led not to the mutual satisfaction of the tenant-buyer and the landlord-seller but to overcrowding, sharing of often insanitary accommodation, bug-infested walls, constant

insecurity and misery in domestic life. The reason for
this was that housing was a commodity and, like all
commodities produced under capitalism, it was there
to be sold and only incidentally to satisfy a need. Yet
unlike most other commodities produced to meet basic
needs—such as food and clothing—housing had cer-
tain distinctive qualities: it was durable, having a life
longer than the user, generally 70 to 100 years, and
was fixed. The costs of producing such commodities
were high in relation to the general level of wages of
workers. First, there was the land on which it was
built; not only was land limited and fixed in supply
but it was owned by a few people. Throughout this
period land was still largely in the possession of the
nobility, Church and Crown. Housing and industrialisation had gone hand in hand in creating the towns
and urban concentrations. The combination of the narrow class basis of land ownership, and the necessary
concentration of housing into a limited number of
areas, meant that inflated, monopoly prices were
charged. Added to this were the actual cost of building
and maintaining the house or tenement including
wages, materials, contribution to wear and tear of tools
and equipment, various legal costs, and the builder's
profits. It was on this basis that the landlords con-
fronted the tenants in determining the rent and the
particular balance in "the relation between supply and
demand existing at the moment" decided the
outcome.[23]

Given the costs of housing and the restriction of wages
to the costs of maintaining and reproducing the mass
of workers and their families, which was the very basis
of capital's survival and growth, the outright purchase
by workers of their housing was just not possible. It
had to be acquired piecemeal by renting from a landlord. Buying the house with a loan to be paid off over
the working lifetime of the individual was out of the
question except in the most exceptional of circumstances. Even the private landlord was often a mortgagee, having borrowed money from a building
society or bank. Here, then, was a commodity which
had to be always in scarce supply even if there were

more dwellings than households to be housed. For if at any particular moment in time rents were determined by the interplay of tenant and landlord in the market for accommodation, over time those rents had to cover both the original costs and the current maintenance costs of the property, as well as give the landlord a return for his money comparable to what he could get in other forms of investment such as government stocks and bonds.

Finance capital

The breakdown in production of the 1930s affected capitalism deeply throughout the world. It hastened the regrouping and organisation of production and finance under the control of big capital and in close partnership with the state. It was the phase of monopoly capital: of enormous companies active across national boundaries in their industrial and financial pursuits, yet working even more closely with an expanding and increasingly interventionist state. This change in the overall form of capital, from small-scale competitive to large-scale monopolistic, signalled the death of 'the rentier petit bourgeoisie. Indeed, it is customary to write the history of housing in the 20th century as a lament for a private landlordism facing extinction. It is remarkable how quickly the dominant figure of the second half of the 19th century and the early decades of the 20th, the small private landlord, was eclipsed. Before World War I nine out of ten people lived in privately rented accommodation, and the overwhelming amount of the housing stock was in the hands of the private landlord. Today less than 15% of the housing stock is in the hands of individual private landlords. (See figure 1). In their place stands the much more shadowy and complex figure of finance capital.

Finance capital is capital: it arises from the unpaid labour of the production process. Yet its main area of activity is not industry but lending to governments and private companies and providing services such as insurance, pensions, hire purchase and mortgages. The activities of finance capital are located in a small

Figure 1
National distribution of major forms of tenure
(Source: *Housing Policy: a Consultative Document,
Technical volume section 1, HMSO, 1977*)

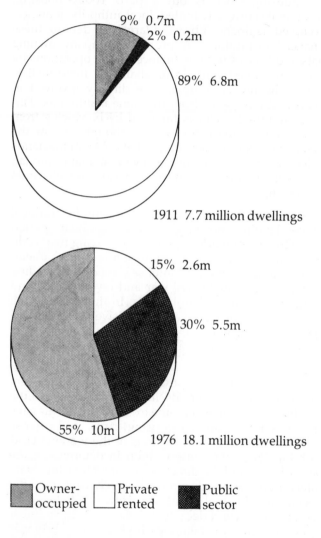

9% 0.7m
2% 0.2m
89% 6.8m

1911 7.7 million dwellings

15% 2.6m
30% 5.5m
55% 10m
1976 18.1 million dwellings

■ Owner-
 occupied
☐ Private
 rented
■ Public
 sector

number of financial institutions: banks, building societies, insurance companies and pension funds. Since World War II these institutions have come to dominate the ownership of land and property of which the housing stock is but a part. Today housing, whether it is privately rented, local authority or owner-occupied, is financed by, and largely in debt to, these financial institutions. A property company owning flats and houses to let is financed in its operations by loans and investments in its shares by these institutions. The owner-occupiers are directly involved in loans and mortgages from the same institutions. Finally, the public sector is financed by borrowing from these same sources. So today, although 55% of the housing stock is owner occupied and 30% in the hands of local authorities, the money lenders, finance capital, are the dominant factor in the provision and allocation of housing.

The change from private landlord to institutional money lending encompasses an extraordinary period in the history of world capitalism, involving two world wars, the breakdown in production and mass unemployment of the 30s, and intense class conflict leading in some countries to civil war and revolutionary and counter-revolutionary upheavals. In this country, the General Strike of 1926 was the decisive event in inter-class relations, and the defeat of the working class cleared the political ground for further advances for capital.

In terms of the housing stock, two wars and the Great Crisis meant long periods in which there was little addition to, or renewal of, the existing stock. This gave rise to serious shortages, rising rents, and intense struggles on the part of sections of the working class to bring about state intervention in determining the level of rents and the direct provision of housing. State intervention followed upon and largely confirmed the decline in individual private investment in housing for rent. By the second decade of this century the number of houses built was falling each year and by 1914 was down to 48,000.[24] In the expanding institutions of finance capital the middle classes found more flexible and lucrative sources of investment than housing. Those with savings to invest were putting their money into War Loans, not out of patriotism but for the interest paid. The traditional propertied middle class was on the wane.

The need to finance the 1914–1918 War by increasing the national debt fuelled the growth of finance capital dramatically. "Compared with the pre-war position, the national debt increased from 1/40 to 1/4 of the total private property in the country; the annual interest payments, negligible before the war, rose to over 40% of the budget, and as prices fell in the early 1920s, the real burden of the debt, both on the budget and in more general terms, as payment from the mainly active part of the population to the mainly inactive, became distinctly heavier."[25] The savings of both the old, propertied, and the new, salaried, middle classes were gathered up by the institutions of finance capital.

The pressures of war-time mobilisation of the labour force, shaken by the actions of the workers on the Clyde in 1915 against rising rents, forced the state to intervene and impose controls over both the level of rents and mortgage interest payments. The events of this period encapsulated the fate of the private landlord. On the one hand, he was subject to working class action and pressure mediated through the State in the form of controls over rent levels, and, on the other hand, the beginning of a real growth in financial institutions gathering up the small savings of the middle classes and seeking profitable outlets for investment in Government stocks and bonds and life assurances. The great mass of private landlords that remained increasingly acted as mediators between tenants and finance capital, and in the course of time were gradually squeezed out.

Changes in ownership

In this century there have been important changes in ownership of land. The New Doomsday Survey of 1873 revealed some seven thousand people owning "four-fifths of the nation's land".[26] At the heart of this private ownership of land were the great private estates of the aristocracy—some two hundred families. Many of these families prospered from the growth in towns and industry in the 19th century. However, in this century, in the inter-war years, a dramatic shift took place in the ownership of land. In the space of about ten years following the First World War, between 6 and 8 million acres of land changed hands. Agricultural depression and rising mineral taxes pressured the nobility into selling land, particularly their urban holdings. Such transfers were assisted by the removal in 1925 of "the last legal constraints on the sale of inherited land and property. . ."[27] Despite the scale of the turnover in land the aristocracy managed to retain a large share of this country in their personal possession, and to this day still own some 30% of the total acreage, although it is now mostly agricultural land. There are exceptions, notably in London, where the nobility still own land on a sizeable scale: the Duke of Westminster, Earl of Cadagon, Duke of Bedford and Viscount Portman are among them. Also to be included amongst this category of traditional landowners are the Crown and Church, which between them own 430,000 acres of land, including extremely valuable urban holdings.[28]

The break-up and sale of the urban holdings of the aristocracy in the inter-war years opened the way to investment in such land by the expanding institutions of finance capital: the banks, life insurance companies and building societies. The banks and insurance companies financed, through loans and mortgages, the purchase and development of urban land for both commercial and residential purposes. Much of the actual development was undertaken by property companies and individual entrepreneurs. Property companies have existed since the 1860's, but it was between the Wars that they came into their own, developing shopping parades and department stores as well as residential estates. For the traditional landowners, the aristocracy and gentry, land was a source of wealth, social position and political power. For the new investors, land was first and foremost a financial asset. Compared to some investments it offered little risk, plus a guaranteed payment in the form of rents, and, with rising rents and appreciating land values, it was inflation-proof and offered the possibility of large financial gains.

In the years immediately following World War I, despite the urgings of the Government of the day, there was a continuing shortfall in house building. In order to make good this situation, there was for the first time in the 1920s a significant programme of local authority slum clearance and house building. Houses were built with bathrooms and sculleries for working class families to rent, although in the early estates in London there was a preponderance of what then were better-off white collar workers moving into local authority housing.

Taking the inter-war years as a whole, the most significant change was in the growth of owner occupation. This was made possible by the growth in the number and size of building societies. Building societies existed throughout the 19th century. In mid-century they were transformed from savings clubs for the building of houses into permanent saving and loan institutions: the Woolwich Equitable, Abbey National and Halifax were all established in and around 1850, but their activities were small in scale. It was from the 1930s onwards that building societies came to play a growing role in individual owner occupation. These societies specialised in lending money for house purchase. The loan was for a fixed period and was secured against the property purchased. Repayment was usually in the form of monthly instalments. At this time hundreds of new societies were formed, adding to the number of older ones of longer standing. They offered a secure investment for the savings of the middle class, especially those not already associated with small property ownership.

Successive governments actively promoted the building societies so as to encourage private purchase of housing and give citizens a "stake in the country". The middle classes were mobilised to both invest their savings and to buy their own homes. The much publicised Building Society Movement, crowned by the appearance of the Prince of Wales at the International Building Societies Congress in London in June 1933, acted as a counter to working class pressure for public housing.[29]

The increasing availability of mortgages helped prime a boom in the building of small houses costing between £500 and £600 and occasionally less.[30] Between the Wars, 2.7 million houses were built by private builders for private purchase and rent. At the same time 1.2 million were built for local authority renting. A further ½ million dwellings were put up with the aid of public subsidies. Towards the end of the thirties a rough balance between the number of dwellings and households was achieved for the first time since the industrial revolution. Almost a quarter of this stock was owner-occupied and just over a tenth was local authority housing. Roughly two thirds was still in the private rented sector, although now the property companies were looming larger among the mass of individual private landlords.[31]

Property development

The full importance of the changes in land ownership and the expansion of finance capital into the funding of commercial and residential property revealed itself from 1945 onwards. The impact on urban life was every bit as great as the road widenings and railway construction of mid and late Victorian times. Whole city centres and vast areas of residential accommodation were razed to the ground, neighbourhoods were torn apart, and millions of people were uprooted and regrouped. For many it was the Second Blitz, although this time it was not the result of Nazi bombardment but a programme of demolition carried out by an alliance of financiers, property developers and the local agents of the state. It was a case of profitable development under public guidance. At the end of the War it was necessary to make good the extensive damage to commercial and residential property. Half a million houses were completely destroyed or damaged beyond repair, a further quarter of a million dwellings suffered serious war damage and another three and a quarter million needed some making good as a result of the bombing. But the long property boom of the post-war years, which produced the biggest changes in our towns and cities since Victorian times, was not simply the outcome of making good the destruction of the 1939–45 war; it was rather the consequence of a more profound change in the whole social process of capitalist production. In capital's monopoly phase, production was on a much more integrated and extended scale. This affected not only factory organisation, the move to larger units and the decline of the small inner city workshop, but also retailing, new enlarged outlets, warehousing and transport, financing, such as personal insurance and hire purchase, and professional and personal services. The demand was for more and more office accommodation, purpose built, to meet the new organisational forms of routinised clerical labour. The demand for commercial property came from the public sector too, where growth in state activities in the nationalised industries, health, education, housing and social services involved new and extended forms of administration. In terms of both physical quantity and monetary value the post-war boom was primarily a matter of commercial property—housing was secondary.

The development of commercial property transformed the centres of most cities: new office and shopping complexes, entertainment and leisure centres were built, ringed by new housing estates and speculative private housing ventures. In the alliance of financiers, developers and local authorities, the limited resources of labour, land and building materials were drawn into the profitable commercial development. Housing, except for the more luxury speculative developments, took second place. The rent per square foot of a dwelling, for whatever social class, just could not compete with what was being charged for office or retailing space. The difference was anything from three to fifteen times as much for commercial as opposed to residential property. The fierce competition for land to develop pushed up land values and the rates and rents of the inner urban areas. London and the South-East were at the centre of these developments. The big multi-national companies, overseas banks and central government departments outbid each other in the search for office space. In the 60s and 70s offices mushroomed throughout central London. The orchestrator of these developments was the property developer. At the height of the boom it was estimated that one hundred developers made one million pounds or more each. The developer acted "as an intermediary between landowners, estate agents, planners and the financial institutions".[32] Through secret and astute dealings he assembled key sites in the area to be developed, often helping to generate the blight of a neighbourhood and so necessitating its eventual development. Tolmers Village in central London was a vivid example of the efforts of the developer's hidden burrowings. He was the figure who carried through the negotiations with the local authority, playing off land for housing in order to gain the planning consent for the commercial development. It was as go-between that the developer had to succeed, for all the time he was working on behalf of the banks, insurance companies and pension funds, assembling the finance, and in this acted "as an agent for finance capital".[33]

The real movers of events were not the villains of the piece, Charles Clore, Joe Levy and Harry Hyams, but private financial institutions. The interest of these institutions was purely financial. The life insurance companies and pension funds (allowed for the first time in 1955 to invest in land and property) generally require long-term assets to cover their liabilities. They do not borrow and lend for short periods, as banks generally do, but deal over much longer periods. Today, land and property are financial assets. The value of either is determined by the price at which it can be sold in the open market, which in turn is related to the level of rents and their rate of growth. "For example, the offices at Euston Centre owned by Stock Conversion and Investment Trust (Mr Joe Levy's company) rose in value from around £15 million in 1964 to nearly £74 million in 1972. Mr Levy did not actually have to do anything to bring about this rise in value. It all stemmed from the growth of rent levels in the area from £1.75 to £6.50 per sq. ft. . . ." and the general expectation of further increases.[34] Renewal and refurbishing of the housing stock took second place. House building costs were drawn into the price spiral of the most spectacular ever property boom. War damage, strategic areas blighted by the property developers, and neighbourhoods zoned by the local planning authority for redevelopment, eventually were laid waste and in the process millions of people displaced. They were rehoused in clusters of tower blocks in the inner urban areas and in the encampments of the new towns, such as Stevenage and Harlow in the South and Peterlee and Kirkby in the North. Millions were moved by economic compulsion to find work and accommodations they could afford. Those who out of age, sentiment and love were unwilling to move were cajoled, bullied or tricked into leaving their homes and the security of familiar streets. The misery was long drawn-out and widespread. Individuals and families were separated from each other, uprooted and dispersed. Many resisted, formed tenants associations and sought to make public their plight. The upheaval in family and neighbourhood relations, and the hurt and anguish it caused, were condoned by public officials and representatives as regrettable consequences of progress.

The experience of a Cardiff resident, moved to a new block of flats, runs deep in an entire generation: "The 76 year old lady said she was on tranquillisers. She woke at 5 every morning and didn't know what was going to happen. She had a heart complaint. She had lost a stone and a half. She would never get used to a flat—couldn't sleep with people above and down below her. Her friend who had just moved into a flat had got to step into the bath to open a window and she was 50. Her friend over the road was the same—all of a tremble. Everything was so handy in town—if anything happened to her people were there to hear you and see you and look after you".[35]

But the housing stock had grown. In the 1960s, for the first time, the number of dwellings surpassed the number of households. Estimates suggest an excess of half a million dwellings over households by the end of the 1970s. The primary reason for this state of affairs was the extensive building of new estates by the local authorities. They had not merely supplemented the activities of private speculative house building but had extended the housing stock beyond the limits imposed by the open market in housing. Few towns of any size had less than 20 per cent of their flats and houses in the hands of the council. The excess of dwellings over households, however, does not resolve the housing shortage. Some of the property is empty because of its physical state of disrepair and is awaiting demolition, or is empty awaiting speculative development or sale with vacant possession at a price beyond the reach of most workers. Other dwellings are technically not empty but are the second or third homes of the upper, and more prosperous middle, classes. Indeed, millions continue to live in sub-standard or over-crowded dwellings and homelessness is an experience for hundreds of thousands of men, women and children.

The estimated housing stock in England and Wales in 1975 was some 18 million dwellings. At least four out of five of these dwellings were houses: either terraced, semi-detached or quite separate. About 1/3 were built before the First World War, and less than half, about 45%, are of post-war construction. The more recent acquisition to the housing stock is more or less equally divided between the two main tenure groups; owner-occupiers and council tenants. The private rented sector is increasingly concentrated in the older property, 76% of it being pre-1914. (See figure 1.)

Since the War some of the worst sub-standard property has either been demolished or renovated, but still the problem does not go away: poor housing, over-crowding and homelessness remain part of the daily lives of millions. In 1976, 1 out of 20 dwellings were officially declared unfit for human habitation, although most were occupied. 1 out of 12 have no inside lavatory. 1 out of 20 have no fixed bath in the

Age distribution of housing stock by tenure:
England and Wales 1975 (figures in millions)

	Owner-occupation	Local authority & New Towns	Private landlords & miscellaneous	TOTAL
Pre-1914	3.4	0.3	2.2	5.9
1914-44	2.7	1.2	0.3	4.2
1945 and after	3.8	3.7	0.4	7.9
	9.9	5.2	2.9	18.0

taken from *Housing Policy: A Consultative Document*, p. 142.

bathroom. 1 out of 9 have no hot water supply to the bath, hand basin and sink. In short, 10% of the housing stock is below the minimum standards. Official estimates say that 1 in 10 households live in sub-standard or unfit housing. A further 1 in 13 live in shared accommodation and are overcrowded. These figures represent an improvement over the situation prevailing in the 1960s. As regards empty property, however, the number of dwellings standing idle is on the increase. Figures for 1971 reveal 640,000 empty dwellings, 100,000 of which have never been lived in.[36]

Today, these problems of poor housing stock and overcrowding are to be found in most towns and cities, but London is worst off in these respects. Unlike the rest of the country, where there are more dwellings on average than households, this is not the case with London, especially in its inner areas. Taking the 32 inner London boroughs as a whole there is at best a rough balance between dwellings and households, but compared to the rest of the country there is a higher proportion of empty property, the housing stock is older and there is a higher proportion of people living in sub-standard and over-crowded accommodation.

Forms of tenure

The real feature of significance is the change in the ownership of this stock. At the beginning of the century most housing, roughly 90%, was in the hands of the private landlord. By the 1970s the picture is quite different: 55% of all dwellings are now owner-occupied, almost entirely mortgaged by building societies (over 80%) and to a much lesser extent by local authorities, banks and life insurance companies. Building society finance dominates the private housing market. Changes in the availability of funds and the interest rates charged affect both house purchase and its private construction. According to the Registrar General of Friendly Societies, building societies grew during the building boom of the 1960s by £6,400 million or 222%.[37] "In 1969 the assets of the two largest societies, the Halifax and Abbey National, alone exceeded the assets of the whole movement ten years earlier. At the same time, individual societies have grown more powerful through a series of mergers. The number of societies has been reduced from 2,286 in 1900 to 726 in 1960 and 382 in 1975. Of these societies, 18 are dominant: they grant about 80 per cent of all building society mortgages and operate about 75 per cent of the movement's branches".[38] It is to these institutions of finance capital that the bulk of owner-occupiers are indebted.

A further 30% of the stock is now publicly owned, mostly local authority housing. The privately rented sector has shrunk to less than 15%. The traditional individual private landlord owning a few properties is fast disappearing. The landlords of importance in this sector today are the property companies, the Crown and Church, and housing associations, a product of Victorian philanthropy, recently given the kiss-of-life by a Labour Government seeking to stave off the complete collapse of the private rented sector.

The two principal forms of tenure today are council and owner-occupation. Although often thought of as constituting radically differing alternatives to rights of occupancy, they share a common subordination to the dictates of private finance and each is supported by public subsidies. Local authority housing is not self-financing, but is largely based upon money borrowed either directly from the capital market or from the Public Works Loan Board which acts as an intermediary between loan capital and the individual local authority. So expansion of the public sector also means increasing indebtedness and dependence on private financial institutions. By the mid-70s, 68% of local authority housing costs were in fact interest charges. No other local authority service is so burdened. For education and roads the interest charges on monies borrowed amounted to 9% and 16% respectively.[39] The support given to council housing through the rates and central government grants and the tax relief on mortgage payments are in reality not subsidies to individual households at all but payments of public money to private loan capital, the money lenders. Finance capital is now the dominant figure in housing.

Chapter 2
Family, home and state

Housing and social relations

Houses are more than simply places of shelter. They fulfil specific social and individual needs which determine not only their location but also their internal arrangements and shape. In their modern form, houses are the product of this society, resting as it does on the foundation of capitalist production, and are shaped by the general arrangement of social relations determining the processes of labour and social life. In mature capitalist society, housing encloses an extraordinarily vital dimension of social life: the generation and daily reproduction of the various social groups of capitalist society. This involves a complex range of tasks: cooking, laundry, basic health care and the nurturing of children, which, taken together, constitute domestic labour. Houses are places in which people work, relax, love and suffer.

To understand housing today and the uses to which it is put, we must distinguish two aspects of capitalist social relations. The first is the specific form of the sexual division of labour which makes domestic labour women's labour, enforcing an economic dependency of women on men. The second is that the self-contained dwelling sets itself against the social (i.e. collective) satisfaction of basic needs. Cooking, child-care and housework tend to be largely the individual concern of women. Domestic labour as a private activity helps enforce the psychological subordination of women to men. This individualised form of satisfying basic needs is important in a society in which production depends on the sale of ever-greater quantities of commodities. It is not simply a matter of the immediate needs of living being catered for by electric mixers, pre-packaged food, refrigerators and washing machines, but also that these same things are meant to offer meaning and personal gratification. Children are prepared for the world of consumerism by being held in a suspended state of childhood with the aid of toys, television and a schooling completely isolated from production. In order to get away from it all there is the most profitable of all capitalism's commodities in the twentieth century, the family car. People are exhorted to work all the harder to *produce* these commodities, and the *consumption* of these same commodities is offered in return as an escape from the tedium and nervous strain of daily labour. The circle is complete.

But this capitalist ideal of private home life centred on consumption hides a darker reality of poverty and isolation. The problems arising from such home-centred family life are at least gaining medical and social recognition: the serious states of depression associated with the isolation of the housewife in the home and its attendant problems of drug-dependency and alcholism, the fact that three out of four child murders are by the hand of the parents and that the majority of killings are family affairs. Domestic life is the source of much anxiety and anguish. To understand how this isolation of the immediate family unit has come about it is necessary to retrace the history of housing as a place for home life.

During the period of industrial capital's dominance, the most elementary shelter was provided close to the new places of work. Under the rentier petit bourgeoisie, the state undertook to provide the infra-structure of housing-piped water and the disposal of sewerage and refuse. Then, with the transformation of housing finance under the growth of monopoly capitalism the state undertook, through a system of subsidies, to directly and indirectly help in the provision of individual dwellings. For the emerging Labour Party, municipal housing offered the possibility of solving the housing problem, of providing a decent home to each and all, irrespective of ability to pay. When Mrs Ramsey Macdonald defined socialism as the "State of the Homes" she echoed the thoughts of many Social Democrats.[1]

From family to factory

In the early decades of the formation of capitalist industry, the massing together of workers into towns was a spontaneous process. The new concentrations of workplace and dwellings contained a change in the process of production of profound social significance, yet one barely perceived at the time: namely, the displacement of the family as the unit of production by the factory. Before capitalism, the family as a whole, whether peasant or artisan, participated in production. Work and domestic life were in no way sharply and clearly separated. It was production in its capitalist form, of wage-labour commanded by capital, which eventually destroyed this unity of family and labour— not at one blow but as the outcome of the first great pioneering phase of industrialisation, from the 1780s to the mid-19th century.

In the early stages, production was still performed on the basis of a simple handicraft technology, and the capitalist either handed out work to be performed by the family in the home (whether it was weaving, spinning, ribbon or hat-making), or the whole family was brought into the mill or mine. In either case the family was engaged together in the labour process. In both cases the paternal authority of the family was incorporated into the discipline of the labour process. This twin development of taking work to the family or bringing the whole family into the factory was very much a part of the early expansion of cotton manufacture, the mainspring of the industrial revolution. In both cases, engaging the whole family in the labour process was a carry-over from an earlier epoch of non-mechanised and localised production based on the labour of peasants and artisans. Involving the whole family eventually proved inappropriate to the new mechanical processes of large-scale industry generated by capitalism and the practice withered away. Outwork declined throughout the decades of the 30s and 40s until it was of marginal economic importance. A succession of legislative measures regulating child labour helped break up family employment in the factories and encouraged the use of new labour-saving machinery. In a matter of decades the family was eliminated from the labour process, and the new industrial towns, while massing men, women and children together as never before, at the same time concealed a deepening separation between workplace and home. The consequence of this split was a radical transformation in the relations pertaining between men, women and children, the family, and the place of the home in social life.

Under capitalism it is not use but exchange that rules the production process, and the principle of the equal exchange of commodities comes to dominate all aspects of social and cultural life: "money counts", as the saying goes. In this early period industrial capital itself was usually involved in the construction of workers' dwellings. The buildings were there to provide shelter from the elements and proximity to the place of work. The minimum was provided. The use the inhabitants might need and wish to make of their dwellings was of little or no account to the individual capitalist. Even the more general interests of capital as a whole in the physical survival and growth of the labour force were neglected. A recognition of the significance of housing for the stability of social relations and their successful reproduction came much later. It was not until the era of the rentier petit bourgeoisie, the 1850s to the 1930s, that the upper classes, the titled and wealthy, came to recognise the general importance of housing conditions and put stress on the home as the source of physical and moral well-being, and that the state actually came to intervene on a significant scale in the housing conditions of the masses. Finally, it was not until the present phase of monopoly capital that large sections of the working class actually got a home of their own in the form of a dwelling that was self-contained.

Re-uniting the family

The early factory towns and mining villages were places of ill-health. The spontaneous expansion of capitalist production undermined the physical well-being of the workers and endangered their capability for

reproducing the labour force. The evident physical
deterioration of the workers, both through injury and
sickness, the lowering of life expectancy for male and
female operatives, and the high infant mortality
amongst women working in factories, slowly became
matters of public concern. Estimates for one of the
typical new industrial towns, Oldham, revealed that
one worker's child in five died before its first birthday.
One female worker in seven died while in the age
group 25 – 34 (mostly from tuberculosis). One miner
in every five could expect to be killed during a normal
working life.[2] Tuberculosis, typhus and scrofula were
major causes of death affecting men, women and
children.

The individual capitalist showed scant concern. Children were maimed. Men and women died in their
twenties and thirties. Their places were easily filled;
no worker was indispensable in the new factories.
However, from a social point of view there was the
danger that the immediate producers would not be
reproduced in sufficient numbers. The factories
appeared to be devouring their life blood—hence the
hesitant and gradual intervention by the state, first to
eliminate child labour and later to provide protection
for women as the potential mothers and rearers of
new generations of workers. As early as 1784, "an
epidemic of disease in a cotton mill had . . . drawn
attention to the conditions of factory children".[3] Even
so, the first Factory Act in 1802 was designed not to
eliminate, but to improve the conditions of, child
labour. It took a further fifty years before child labour
was eliminated.

The state was not acting out of benevolence but as a
result of the need, made public by the resistance of
the workers themselves, to keep in bounds the particular interests of competing capitals—to curb their
"wildest excesses".[4] The Factory Acts and the Factory
Inspectorate were the first conscious effort at regulating what was otherwise a spontaneous process of
industrial development. Although the state is an
apparatus of coercion and control and as such serves
the interests of capital, it does so in relation to stabil-

ising the social relations of capitalist society as a whole. Hence its intervention in the factory was not a challenge to capital's command of the labour process, but a curbing of the most destructive aspects of the exploitation of wage-labour. Marx says of this first "conscious and methodical reaction" on the part of the state: "What could possibly show better the character of the capitalist mode of production, than the necessity that exists for enforcing upon it, by Acts of Parliament, the simplest appliances for maintaining cleanliness and health?"[5] Capitalist society, unlike the preceding feudal social order, is based on social relations that are "freely" entered into by the individual. The labour of the wage-earner is not subject to physical coercion as was the peasant's by the lord or priest. Wage-labour is unbounded labour. The only compulsion to work is economic necessity, otherwise the worker is free to choose his employer. Because of this open and fluid nature of social relations, the state expanded the institutional arrangements for preserving the unity of capitalist society. The widespread use of the army, courts, gallows and prisons in the early decades of the Industrial Revolution was supplemented by workhouses, hospitals and schools as less rigid custodial institutions for the out-of-work, the chronically sick and the dependent young. The more circumspect elements of the upper classes recognised the importance of keeping the family intact as the lynch-pin in the extremely fluid and evolving relations of the new capitalist social order.

The new industrial towns were rife not only with disease but also with crime and rebelliousness. Gradually the attention of Parliament was drawn to the question of the workers' physical health and moral well-being. The expulsion of children from the factories posed once again the question of the family. The solution to the problem of their care was seen to lie in the hands of the bearer of the children, the mother. This partly accounts for the legislation protecting women in employment which followed the ending of child labour. The first legislation aimed specifically at protecting women was the 1842 Mines Act which excluded women and colliery employment.[6]

As the family lost its place in the production process the dwelling became the place for recreating its unity and, to the enlightened bearers of capital's interests, was the safeguard for the continuance of the species. The existence of the family was no longer based upon a shared labour but a common hearth. With work providing no more meaning than a money-wage, the home came more and more to be the source of all comfort and care for the workers and their children. Capitalism in its development confirmed the women's responsibility for the well-being of the father, the principal earner, and their children, and did so in the context of the increasing separation of home-life from work. This isolation of the home from work heralded the economic dependency of women in marriage and their exclusive responsibility for domestic labour. The early dwellings of the workers provided little more than elementary shelter, and gave no real space for the new form of family life produced by capitalism. Modern industry produced its counterpart: home as a refuge from work. But the production of dwellings sufficient and suitable for such a home life was something beyond the capacity of profit-seeking capital. The gap between the idea and the reality, as far as the masses were concerned, revealed itself in the observations of a contemporary well imbued with the values of the new social order:

"It is no uncommon thing, in a room of twelve feet square or less, to find three or four families styed together (perhaps with infectious diseases among them) filling the space day and night—men, women and children, in the promiscuous intimacy of cattle. Of these inmates, it is mainly superfluous to observe that in all offices of nature they are gregarious and public, that every instinct of personal and sexual decency is stifled, that every nakedness of life is uncovered".[7]

Towards the middle of the 19th century it was quite common for whole families to live in one room and for a ten-roomed house to have 45 to 60 people living in it. In Liverpool by 1840, 30,000 people, one-fifth of the working class, lived in 7,800 "inhabited cellars".[8]

Insanitary conditions

The regulation of factory life made the working conditions of the immediate producers more tolerable, but failed to check the epidemics blighting the new industrial heartlands of capitalism. Typhoid, tuberculosis, cholera, diphtheria, tetanus and plague were the scourge of town life. Ignorance and indifference gave way in the middle of the 19th century to a growing concern and public encouragement to tackle the problem. Cholera was the great fear, "striking terror into the minds of the middle and upper classes. . .". It first hit Britain in 1831–2, and returned in 1848–9, 1854 and 1867. It struck quickly, was extremely contagious and resulted in many deaths. Unlike typhus it was not simply "a poor man's disease" and public administrative action was urgently demanded.[9]

As a consequence, attention was shifted from the workplace to the living quarters. The success of the Factory Acts and Factory Inspectorate in curbing some of capital's worst excesses in production was followed in the latter half of the century by a comparable series of Public Health Acts and the formation of an Inspectorate of medical health officers to investigate and enforce regulations in the area of domestic life. In keeping with capital, the initial concern was with "the cost of pauperism". This led to the first investigations of "epidemic disease and its relation to poverty". The urgency given to these investigations, however, did not come from "the fear of the spread of infection".[10] The focus was on the insanitary conditions of working class housing. In the 1840s, "soon after the beginning of the civil registration of births and deaths (1837), there was evidence to show that the death rate was much higher in towns where housing conditions were worst".[11] This was the start of a large number of official enquiries and reports, beginning with the *Inquiry into the Sanitary Condition of the Labouring Population of Great Britain* in 1842. This report exposed the appalling conditions in which the working class and the poor were housed. It outlined the general economic and social costs that such conditions gave rise to. The Report was at pains to establish that general insanitary conditions, the physical state of the dwellings and over-crowding were preventing the existence of a clean and healthy family life. Example after example of the consequences of such conditions were put forward. If the dwellings were not in a physical condition to be kept clean, character alone would not suffice. The Report argued that however good the wife, even if she "has had a good industrial training in the well regulated household of persons of a higher condition", it would prove of no avail if the dwelling was in such poor physical state that it could not be kept clean and orderly. The "habits of neatness, order, and cleanliness . . ." would not in themselves suffice to achieve the standards of family life that were required.[12] But if women were receiving no domestic training at all, then the problem of the mismanagement of the home was serious indeed. The Committee of Physicians and Surgeons at Birmingham expressed clearly the petit bourgeois male's viewpoint on the matter of "depraved domestic habits":

"The improvidence of which we are speaking is to be traced in very many instances to extreme ignorance on the part of the wives of these people. The females are from necessity bred up from their youth in the workshops, as the earnings of younger members contribute to the support of the family. The minds and morals of the girls become debased, and they marry totally ignorant of all these habits of domestic economy which tend to render a husband's home comfortable and happy; and this is very often the cause of the man being driven to the alehouse to seek that comfort after his day of toil which he looks for in vain by his own fireside. The habit of a manufacturing life being once established in a woman, she continues it, and leaves her home and children to the care of a neighbour or of a hired child, sometimes only a few years older than her own children, whose services cost her probably as much as she obtains for labour".[13]

The Report was put before Parliament in the summer of 1842, a critical period for inter-class relations: unemployment was high, destitution abounded and social protest was widespread. The Chartists, the first working class political movement of national proportions, organised a general strike.

The combination of epidemic disease and social unrest had given urgency to Chadwick's compilation and presentation of the Report. Even so it was not until 1848 that the Public Health Act was passed and a measure of state responsibility taken for safeguarding the health of the population. The deliberations of Parliament were slow and the formulation of legislative proposals cautious. Every care was taken to avoid seriously impinging on the rights of private property. The execution of the powers bestowed on local authorities by the Act required of the medical officers of health caution and tact in their exercise. It was the age in which the rentier petit bourgeoisie came to dominate housing. This class was the bearer of the modern idea of the home—"the dwelling place as a home, composed of different rooms with different functions, and the idea of family life as a private and basically child-centred affair"[14]—as its ideal. At the same time this class was the principal owner of the housing stock with its mass of insanitary and overcrowded dwellings. To this class the rights of private property were absolutely essential to individual freedom and the bedrock of the successful individualism preached in Victorian times. State intervention into the conditions of housing sought to involve as little interference with these property rights as possible. It achieved this by bringing into state ownership and supervision not the dwellings themselves but the infra-structure of housing: the drains, the water supply, street paving and lighting and rubbish disposal. Numerous acts were passed during the Victorian period to improve the sanitary conditions of working class housing and encourage action in those areas and districts where conditions were particularly hazardous to health. Many towns had their own Health Committees to oversee and help improve local water supplies, drainage and sewerage disposal as well as inspect food and milk supplies. In 1869 the Royal Sanitary Commission summarised the minimum sanitary conditions necessary for a decent social life. It encompassed the supply of water, "sewerage, streets and highways, housing, the removal of refuse, consumption of smoke, public lighting, inspection of food, provision for the burial of the dead, registration of death and sickness. . ."[15]

The legislative landmark for housing was the Public Health Act of 1875. This Act laid down standards for the building of houses which governed the construction of a large part of the housing stock still in use today. The Act aimed at ensuring that houses were of a solid construction and generally had a piped water supply, waterborne sewerage and proper ventilation.[16] In the same year further legislation gave local authorities the powers to demolish insanitary slums. Such slum clearance could be pursued either because it could be shown that the health of the inhabitants of the dwellings was at risk or from consideration of the possible dangers of such properties to the health of the public at large. The Act provided the local authorities with the powers to compulsorily acquire insanitary properties within their boundaries. After the acquisition the properties could be demolished and new houses built but only for sale to private owners. The petit bourgeois possession of the housing stock was not immediately affected.

These were the powers under which "the infamous and fever-ridden courts and alleys of central London (such as St. Giles, Clare Market and Wild's Rents)" were cleared. Slum clearance was undertaken in many of the larger towns. This was the period known to Victorians as the "Age of Improvement". Some local authorities such as Birmingham were anxious to make improvements. The Medical Officer of Health produced a report on a "scheduled area": he described "the narrow streets, houses without back doors or windows, situated both in and out of courts; confined yards; courts open at one end only, and this one opening small and narrow; the impossibility in many instances of providing sufficient privy accommodation; houses and shopping so dilapidated as to be in imminent danger of falling, and incapable of proper repair". He listed what he saw as the consequence of these conditions for both the physical and moral health of the inhabitants: "want of ventilation, want of light, want of proper and decent accommodation, resulting in dirty habits, low health and debased morals on the part of the tenants."[17] He spoke for a morality founded on the private possession of property. The legislation enabling clearance of such slums provided at the same time safeguards for private possession of housing. Slum clearance generally meant eviction for the inhabitants of the area to be improved. "Pushed out from their homes and unable to move far afield or afford the rents of the model dwellings that arose on the sites cleared . . . the evicted thronged into the already crowded back streets and courtyards, where, until the next round of slum clearance or street building, they remained in densely crowded dwellings".[18] The medical officers of health found themselves facing the dilemma of such local agents of the state: to act or not to act, whether it was more humane to apply their powers or not. At that time the situation was one of the inhabitants of the slums being evicted with no provision for rehousing. Many medical officers of health held back from applying their powers at all rigorously. One medical officer of health lamented in 1883: "All improvements recoil on the poor."[19]

For the propertied middle classes of Victorian times, home was seen as the source of moral strength. It fell upon the wife as the home-maker to set an example for all to follow, whatever their material circumstances. Looking back on this period one reformer wrote:

"Moreover, whatever the house reform movement may owe to the exertion of individual and associative effort, to private philanthropy, or the action of public authorities—in the last instance it is woman who makes the home what it is, and we cannot more fitly close . . . than by quoting the well-known passage in Mr. Ruskin's *Sesame and Lilies*, defining in glowing words woman's great mission in the homes of rich and poor alike.

'Wherever a true wife comes, the home is always round her. The stars only may be over her head: the glow-worm in the night-cold grass may be the only fire at her foot; but home is yet wherever she is; and for a noble woman it stretches far round her, better than ceiled with cedar, or painted with vermilion, shedding its quiet light far, for those who else were homeless'."[20]

In more immediate and practical terms, these same middle classes aspired to dwellings with separate staircase for themselves and their servants. In 1881, one in seven of the total employed population were in domestic service, and they were mostly women. While the upper classes had large retinues of servants to staff their estates and town houses, the middle classes employed two, three, or even five servants. In the "privacy" of such homes, the more formal relations of contemporary family life were fashioned and annually celebrated in the rituals of the family Christmas with its tree, cards and exchange of gifts. For the greater part of the working class and the destitute life was quite different. Few had their own separate dwellings, and most lived in shared and over-crowded accommodation. Booth wrote of the "dis-homed multitude, nomadic, hungry, that is rearing an undisciplined population. . . ".[21] On the eve of World War I, while the upper 10% of the population on average possessed two rooms for each member of the family, the poorest 10% were living on average two to a room.

Before the 1930s there was very little direct provision by the local authorities of housing to rent as opposed to private purchase. Efforts to ease the housing shortage and over-crowding centred on encouraging private charitable trusts to provide dwellings to house the very poorest. One of the earliest and most successful was the Peabody Trust formed in 1862. Along with the Guinness Trust set up in 1889 it spearheaded efforts to rehouse the poor by building large blocks of flats noted for their austerity and lack of comfort. By 1914

Peabody had 6,400 dwellings. But this venture in private housing, despite the tax relief which in reality was a hidden form of state subsidy, had but a marginal impact on the housing stock and was quite unable to rent even its austere rooms cheaply enough for the lowest paid. Enid Gauldie concludes that the hope that such private enterprise "could deal with the problems of unsanitary housing, homelessness, and overcrowding . . . perhaps held up the progress towards state-controlled housing for decades. . .".[22]

The era of the rentier petit bourgeoisie in housing saw the municipal provision of the infra-structure of housing, the demolition of some of the worst slums of the nineteenth century and the construction of a good part of our present housing stock. The exceptions were few but notable. One that stood out against the general trend was Liverpool which, with some of the worst slums in the country, built the very first council housing, St. Martins cottages, in 1869. The first such project in London was in Battersea in 1892. But these projects were few and far between, and were exceptions to the general rule of non-involvement by the state in the actual provision of housing for rent. By the outbreak of World War I these exceptions had accumulated to the extent that almost 2 per cent of dwellings were in the hands of local authorities, and so remained marginal to the housing needs of the great mass of the workers.

An end to squalor

The necessity of maintaining war-time mobilisation brought about the first open and direct involvement of the state in the provision of housing. In the heat of the War, in 1915, a critical point in the housing shortage was reached amongst the families of the munition workers on the Clyde. Landlords were taking advantage of the wartime situation and charging what the market would bear. Agitation over rent rises grew throughout 1915.

"The situation was worst in the Govan and Fairfields wards, where, by October 1915, rents were 12½% to

23% up on the July level. During the summer of 1915, *Forward*, the ILP weekly paper, reported a whole series of rent strikes, growing in volume towards the autumn. The movement was particularly strong in Goven where a woman's housing committee . . . organised constant propaganda meetings (including factory gate meetings), rent strikes and physical resistance to evictions . . . By October 30th a general strike was in progress. The climax came on November 17th, when to overcome the physical resistance to evictions the factors (landlords' agents) summoned eighteen before the Small Debts Court, intending to get the increased rent impounded from the wages at the source. A demonstration of women outside the Court was joined by all the men from five Govan, Partick and Whiteinch shipyards, and the Coventory Ordnance works in Scotstoun. The other munitions factories are represented, if at all, by deputations. Up to 15,000 people surged around the court house."[23] The Sheriff decided against the factors and the next day the Government announced a Bill to limit rents to their July 1914 level. From that date onwards rents were never again freely determined by the market. The 1915 Act imposed controls that formed "a major element in the fixing of rents both in the public and private sectors between 1915 and 1972"[24].

The importance of 1915 was that it marked the first open and direct involvement of the state in housing finance. There was to be no going back. The decline of the private landlord and the rise of the modern labour movement and increasing working class political pressure exercised through the newly formed Labour Party necessitated the intervention of the state to ease the housing problem. The end of the First World War had seen a serious housing shortage. Lloyd George's pledge to provide "homes fit for heroes to live in" involved the Government of the day supporting a programme for building of 500,000 houses in three years. But this did not happen, and the estimated shortage rose from 600,000 houses in 1918 to 805,000 in 1921.[25] In 1919 the Housing and Town Planning Act empowered local authorities to survey the needs of their area and make provision for housing where necessary. In 1920 public subsidies were provided to encourage private builders to build for rent or sale. In 1923 subsidies were made available to both local authorities and private builders in order to encourage house building.[26] However, the building of local authority housing progressed slowly and the early estates tended to be inhabited by better off sections of the working class and not those most in need. It was not until the Labour Government of 1929 that encouragement was given to slum clearance and the devising of local programmes of house building to meet general needs. At the same time, through specially devised tax concessions, the state was encouraging individual purchase of dwellings. In the wake of the private landlord the two tenures of increasing importance were to be those of council tenant and mortgagor.

The growth of state involvement in housing was a feature of the emerging era of monopoly capital and the dominance in housing of finance capital. It was the product of a new phase in the development of capitalist society in which production was reorganised on an expanded scale under a more centralised ownership and direction. The activity of the state in housing followed upon these changes. It was not simply a matter of the state picking up where capital left off, but rather of mediating the serious social conflicts these changes invoked in the private production and ownership of housing. The passage from competitive capitalism to monopoly capitalism was marked by thirty years of war and social unrest. 1914 to 1945 was a period of world wars, civil strife, revolutionary and counter-revolutionary upheavals in the European heartlands of capitalism. British capitalism came through this historical period of economic and political crisis with its institutions intact. The acute class conflicts that erupted including The General Strike of 1926, were successfully accommodated by the British state.

The state's involvement in housing was part of a larger intervention into social life: the Welfare State. With the ending of the Second World War in 1945 the process of economic and social recovery involved the state in attacking what Beveridge in his influential report termed "the five giants". These were Want, Disease, Ignorance, Idleness and Squalor—each of which was to be met by a specific plan of attack. Want was to be met by a system of social insurance and financial assistance; Disease by the creation of National Health Service; Ignorance by the provisions of the 1944 Education Act; Idleness by full employment and incentives to work; and Squalor by a great programme of house building.

After the shattering experiences of the War, the rebuilding of family life was the focus of these new measures in social welfare. Beveridge was convinced that: "In the next thirty years housewives as Mothers have vital work to do in ensuring the adequate continuance of the British Race and of British Ideals in the world".[27] In the area of social security this meant treating "man and wife as a team" and devising a system of payments supportive of family life. In all areas of social welfare support was given to maintaining the family as the basic social unit. It was the family in its capitalist form, so domestic labour, involving mothering at its centre, was seen principally as women's work.

In housing, the state affected family life directly through control over rent and mortgage levels and through the provision of standards for housing building and their upkeep. The ideal promoted by the middle class and their politicians was of a dwelling closed off in its own garden. The growing building society movement stressed that ownership of such a dwelling gave the individual both personal freedom and a stake in society. This ideal of the self-contained family dwelling, allowing for a home-centred existence, was finally translated and written down for the public sector in the report of a committee headed by Sir Parker Morris under the title of *Homes for Today and Tomorrow*, published in 1961. The Committee believed that "the problem of designing good homes is the same whoever provides them . . . " and that their recommendations should apply "to private enterprise and public authority housing alike".[28] The major recommendations of the report became law for local authority building, but not private, in 1969. Since that date new council dwellings have been said to be of Parker Morris standards. The basic purpose of these standards was to ensure that dwellings were sufficiently spacious and adequately heated for an active and varied home life. Rooms needed to be large enough to be put to more than one use, so that for instance a child's bedroom could be used as a "bed-sit", and kitchens needed to have space for the new equipment: refrigerators and washing machines. There should also be adequate electrical outlets for all the new electrical gadgets— televisions, hair dryers, gramophones and radios— that were features of contemporary capitalism. At last the idea that the dwelling was a home, and should provide the space for a full family life, was given legal recognition.

A necessary institution

Yet today the ideal of a decent home for one and all is far from being a reality. Despite the official claim that there are more dwellings than households, there is still a "shortage". Homelessness, overcrowding and the use of below standard and unfit accommodation are widespread. The excess dwellings are either in the wrong place, or are far too expensive for those in need, or await major repairs or demolition. The lowest paid and the out of work are in no position to rent or buy a dwelling even when a surplus exists. The situation is highlighted by the post-war influx into Britain of Asian and West Indian immigrants. On arriving they moved to those areas where there was a high demand for semi-skilled and unskilled manual labour and initially entered the one tenure open to them, namely the private rented sector. The new immigrants were excluded from council housing and could not initially manage to buy a property, so they had to rent privately.[29] They tended to concentrate in the oldest and cheapest properties in the decaying inner city areas. Even when they pooled savings with relatives and purchased dwellings themselves it tended to be the older, cheaper properties in the same areas of declining, privately-rented accommodation. Immigrants housed their own families and kin or in turn rented out or did both. The availability of accommodation and the cultural need to keep together in a foreign environment helped to create the characteristic concentrations of the immigrant communities. Racial prejudice played its part in funnelling immigrants into particular streets and neighbourhoods even when the purchase of dwellings was possible.

Engels in his study of *The Housing Question* referred to the housing shortage as "a necessary institution" of capitalist society.[30] The dynamic of capitalist production depends on keeping the immediate producers' share of the social product to a historically determined minimum necessary for their maintenance and propagation. This involves capital not only in a struggle over wage levels but in continually re-organising the labour process in order to reduce labour costs. The consequences of this dynamic of the capital/wage-labour relation are periodic slumps in production and mass unemployment, the elimination from time to time of whole categories of skilled labour, fierce competition for jobs, and an element of permanently and frequently unemployed. The housing shortage, Engels pointed out, is a necessary mechanism in the deployment and redistribution of labour. "Home" just cannot have the same permanency for the mass of workers that it might have for the capitalists.

The "necessary institution", however, contains an irreconcilable contradiction for capitalist society. On the one hand, there exists the need to keep in being a mobile and adaptable labour force, for the labour process is continually being transformed, and, on the other hand, there is the need to keep alive the elementary form of the family, parents and children, as the basic unit of social life. The state is continually involved in uprooting families, stripping away extra-familial ties, virtually isolating the family in its most elementary form, while at the same time trying through its social policy and army of social workers, to keep the family together. The first need results in programmes of slum clearance, new building, rent control and rent de-control. The inner city slums are demolished, those displaced are rehoused in new estates both close at hand and next to new centres of employment, such as the new towns developed in the post-1945 period. Changes in employment and the decay of the housing stock are continuing processes requiring new housing projects and the demolition or refurbishing of existing ones. This process, by which the conditions of shortage and squalor and over-crowding are for ever reproducing themselves, fluc-tuates with the ups and downs of capitalist produc-tion. In periods of war, when materials and labour are mobilised for military purposes, and in times of unem-ployment, when people find it increasingly difficult to keep up rent and mortage payments, homelessness and overcrowding increase. This is so even when, as today, there are more dwellings than there are house-holds. It is in this context that the local authority exercises its allocation policy, grading properties and tenants. The shifts in jobs and labour slowly work themselves through, but not without pain and misery for the individuals and families concerned. The hous-ing shortage is a mechanism through which adjust-ments are made. The waiting list, on which individuals can spend their whole lives, is but one of a number of records of peoples' needs that are compiled. Those requiring rehousing, tenants of old privately rented property, newly formed families, people new to that area, single people old and young, divided families, form the basis of most local authority waiting lists. Some are sifted out for re-housing, others are left to wait and/or encouraged to move away altogether. At the same time the larger local authorities provide tem-porary hostel accommodation, short-life property for the homeless, and old and run-down estates for the poorly paid, the out of work, single parent families and families of immigrant labour. A study of Birming-ham, the largest municipal housing authority in the country, reveals the administrative practices by which the housing shortage is regulated and where the Hous-ing Waiting List is not a queue but a process of screening and excluding the thousands seeking Council accommodation.[31]

A hundred years ago the unskilled and casual workers, the frequently and long-term unemployed, were housed in over-crowded slums, barrack-like lodging houses and workhouses for the utterly destitute. Today the low-paid worker and the family or individual on social security still tend to live in the poorest accommodation on offer. They are crowded into run-down, multi-occupied terraced housing still in the hands of private landlords, living in rooms divided by hardboard, sharing a single lavatory and bath. If in council accommodation, they tend to be in the older property needing modernisation: the "problem estates". The priorities of local authority housing allocation encourages officials to fit the "undesirable tenant" to the hardest-to-let property. Consequently it tends to be the lowest paid, the single parent family, the immigrant worker and the pensioner who is often placed in the poorest accommodation. It is precisely the people most vulnerable and subject to bad housing conditions, those threatened with eviction or homeless or desperately over-crowded, who often receive the lowest priority when considered for rehousing by the local authority. The better accommodation generally goes to families and individuals not being rehoused from the waiting list at all but forced to move as the result of the local authority's modernisation or redevelopment programme. A recent study of immigrant access to council housing in a particular local authority area found that even without the operation of any obvious racial bias in the allocation procedures, the minority groups, because they are already concentrated into the lower paid jobs and the worst of the privately rented housing, "tend to be given inferior accommodation", when they come to be rehoused.[32]

Imposition of bourgeois forms

Housing in its contemporary form cuts across the solidarities engendered in the workplace. "It brutally separates workplace from residence, reinforces family instead of factory relations and isolates the worker as

worker from the worker as consumer".[33] It is not simply a matter of individual home ownership that is at
stake here. Although that particular ideal is strongly
held, even without it the idea of one's own home,
whatever the tenure, encourages individual, private
forms of personal life and satisfaction of basic needs.
The actual success over the past fifty years in providing large sections of the working class with their own
exclusive dwelling, whatever its particular physical
shortcomings, has helped make private the various
activities of child-care, cooking, laundry and entertainment. By so doing it has helped foster the individualist
beliefs of capitalist competition and possession
amongst workers themselves: the sanctity of the home
and the desire, come what may, of keeping up appear-
ances of respectability with neighbours encourages
stoicism in the face of difficulties. These attitudes and
responses are materially underpinned by the widespread indebtedness, through purchase of consumer
durable goods on credit, of the individual family as a
consuming unit. The continuous effort to maintain the
weekly payments on the three-piece suite or car has
become part and parcel of the struggle to maintain a
self-contained family life. So, contrary to the work-
place experience, in their home life people are cut off
from their fellow workers, separated from the rest of
their family and isolated even from their neighbours.
This atomisation and isolation of individuals in home
life is in constant tension with the most immediate
relations of co-operation at the heart of the capitalist
production process and its ancillary activities, and
with the elements of a more open and public social life
still to be found in corner shops, betting shops, laun-
dromats and pubs.

Chapter 3
The production of housing

Housing and labour power

Housing is essential to the physical survival and general well-being of the labour force. At the same time it is a "necessary cost of production"[1]. It is a significant part of the costs of reproducing, both daily and generationally, the mass of the labour force. The higher the general costs of housing, the greater the pressure is likely to be to raise wages. It is estimated that on average one tenth of household expenditure is on rent or mortgage repayments alone, and for the lower paid roughly one fifth.[2] From the point of view of capital, cheaper housing helps reduce the costs of the labour power, the abilities of people to labour, that it must employ and so increases the share of unpaid labour that it commands.

The dynamic of capitalist development involves the continual reduction in that part of society's labours necessary for the successful reproduction of the immediate producers. Thus, for example, the proportion of the total labour force engaged in the production of clothing and food is only a fraction of what was necessary a hundred years ago. While the total value of commodities produced has increased enormously, the value of labour power, as a share of the total, has fallen.

The same considerations apply to the production of housing. A reduction in the amount of society's labour necessary for the production of housing will reduce labour's share in the total wealth produced and capital will gain. Yet despite this apparent advantage to capital, housing is one of the branches of capitalist production that has lagged behind general developments in mechanisation and is still labour intensive. The machinery and techniques of large-scale production have yet to be widely applied in house building.[3]

The building industry

Capital is quite without sentiment, destroying all that stands in the way of its growth. In production, the labour process is continually being transformed and traditional skills and crafts swept away. In building, however, the process appears slower and more pro- tracted than in any other major branch of production. As a result, and in a quite unique way, the past of the building industry is preserved in its present structure, and a sketch of existing arrangements reveals a picture of its history. The co-existence of traditional craft tech- niques and modern materials, family firms and inter- national consortia, casual labour and militant site stewards, are features of a production process that has seen few basic changes in the forms of labour co- operation and methods used when it comes to the construction of dwellings. It is an industry character- ised by low fixed investment in plant and machinery, employment of casual labour, poor and unsafe work- ing conditions and inefficient management. More than any other branch of production it is rife with corrup- tion: at every level of its operations it is oiled with "back-handers". The collapse of the building boom in the mid-70s brought about, in the wake of spreading bankruptcies amongst contractors, a spate of corrup- tion trials involving public officials, private contractors and politicians.

It is not a matter of the industry simply having stag- nated—it has not: some changes have taken place. As in other sectors of capitalist production capital has become concentrated into a few hands. A small num- ber of firms dominate the building industry: Wimpey, Laing, Taylor Woodrow, Tarmac, Costains, Mac- Alpine, and Marchwiel Holdings. These firms have an annual turnover running into hundreds of millions of pounds, and between them count their profits in the tens of millions. At the height of the building boom, in 1970, taken together the trading profits of these seven companies amounted to £47½ million. One of the largest, G. Wimpey & Co., had in 1970 a workforce of 30,000, an annual turnover of £225,000,000 and a trading profit for the year of £11,750,000.[4] Yet at the same time they co-exist with a vast mass of tiny firms. Of the estimated 84,000 firms in operation in 1976, more than three-quarters of them employed fewer than 8 workers apiece.[5] To this day it is an industry into which entry is easy, requiring little capital, and departure is both sudden and common. Thus in 1975, although construction accounted for nearly 12½ per cent of Gross Domestic Product, it accounted for about 20 per cent of all industrial bankruptcies and liquidations.[6] The great majority of those going under are among the small firms.

House building as such is but a part of the activities of this branch of production known as the building or construction industry. Much more important and profitable are the building of roads and industrial and commercial property. The really big firms, such as Wimpey and Laing, are involved in building motorways, docks, airports, oil-rigs, factories, office blocks, shopping centres, warehouses, hotels, exhibition halls, hospitals, schools and colleges, libraries and town halls. No more than 30% of the activity of the industry is house building. This includes not only speculative building of luxury flats and individual houses for the wealthy but also new council estates and the conversion of old housing and general maintenance of the existing stock. The mass of small firms stand in a relation to the giants of construction not unlike that of the back-street repair shop to the large motor manufacturers: patching up the other's product. Many building firms do not build houses as such, or do so only rarely, but are involved as sub-contractors providing specialist skills, or concentrate on converting old properties and in carrying out daily repairs and decorations.

Despite the enormous engineering achievements of the 20th century which produced spectacular developments in the building of roads, bridges, offices, and factories, as an industry it remains in many ways archaic. As early as the 1860s James Hole wrote deploring "the lack of advance in methods of building compared to the rate of introduction of methods of mass production in other industries". What the building industry needed, he said, was an Arkwright.[7] The unevenness of mechanisation and the low level of labour productivity are features of the industry to this day. In the manufacture of building materials—bricks, plasterboard, glass, window frames and stairs, piping and wiring—the techniques of mass production are utilised as elsewhere in production. But when it comes to the actual construction of dwellings the productivity of labour has lagged behind that of manufacturing over a long period of time.[8]

To this day building is an industry characterised by predominantly traditional productive methods: limited on-site mechanisation and the widespread use of casual labour. It is not for want of an Arkwright that this situation persists. Inventiveness is not in short supply in construction. Nor is it the fixed and durable nature of the product that precludes continuous mechanised production. The components of motor cars are often manufactured in one place and assembled in another. Indeed, industrialised building methods do exist but have been only marginally employed in some of the very large post-war local authority housing schemes. The backwardness of the industry is not technically determined as is sometimes suggested.[9] It is not the physical qualities of dwellings, nor their being fixed to the ground, nor the vagaries of the weather that causes the lag. Similar factors have not prevented transformations of the labour process in agriculture. The answer is to be found elsewhere.

The contracting system

The Direct Labour Collective, in their pamphlet *Building With Direct Labour*, point to the contract system as the key to the organisation of the industry and its forms of labour co-operation and methods of work. "Most construction work in Britain is . . . undertaken by private building firms. Sometimes they build speculatively . . . Otherwise, they build to contract. Someone wants construction work done, and a builder contracts to do the work for a price. All public sector building work by construction firms is on a contract basis. Contracting dominates the private construction industry. Without it, the construction industry in Britain would not exist in the form it does today."[10]

The general building firm as a form of enterprise came into existence with the industrial revolution and the building of the towns. Today, as in the past, such firms, whether large or small, tend to operate with low fixed costs, financing their operations through credit and loans, hiring plant and dependent on a readily available supply of cheap unskilled labour. Firms submit tenders for particular projects. The costing is complicated and cannot be done with any real accuracy, particularly when it comes to detailed predictions of prices of materials. One illustration will suffice to indicate the problems involved. "In the case of reinforced concrete buildings, for example, bill items are specified down to the detail of individual columns and beams of different girth. The collective labour of a carpenters' gang building the formwork shuttering for the entire floor may be roughly costed in relation to the floor as a unit of output. It cannot meaningfully be broken down into units which correspond to each beam or column moulded. Likewise with the collective labour of a gang of steelfixers who build reinforcing framework for the carpenters."[11] These tenders are not so much estimates of cost as the price at which the firm is prepared to undertake the job. In theory the process of tendering is secret and competitive although in reality there is much collusion between firms. The firm winning the contract, if it completes the job at a cost below the tender, pockets the excess. The experience and skill of the contractor comes out in the assembling and manipulation of the various elements needed to complete the job. Each job or project involves different materials usually acquired on credit, the hire of plant and the employment of various types of labour at varying stages of the work. The whole operation is both full of risk, upward changes in interest rates on money borrowed and in the prices of materials, and opportunity, savings from skimping and the substituting of lower grade materials and less skilled labour for that originally costed. The essence of the operation is the minimising of labour costs. This is achieved through the employment of casual labour and the bonus system. The employment of labour at different phases of the contract and in varying quantities and skill is the vital regulator of costs that the contractor can actually control.

The contract system of work organisation determines the nature of the building industry. The main contractor both sub-contracts work, such as plumbing or glazing, to specialist contractors and hires labour, perhaps carpenters and steelfixers, at different times when it is needed. In this way either directly or indirectly, via the sub-contractors, an army of workers are temporarily employed. At the heart of this system is the sub-contracting of work on a labour-only basis and the individual worker is supposedly self-employed. Such forms of employment are known as the "Lump". There are four basic varieties: "(1) the sub-contractor . . . employing all its workers on contracts of service; (2) the labour-only gang working under a gang leader who employs the members of the gang; (3) a labour-only gang in which all the members are self-employed, although one may take the lead in negotiating the sub-contract; (4) the self-employed worker who makes his own agreement with the contractor."[12] Workers are paid a lump sum, hence the name, for their labour. Such payment offers scope for avoiding paying tax and insurance cover, despite the introduction in recent years of automatic tax-deduction and other measures intended to prevent this.

The contracting system and the network of sub-contractors and "self-employed" workers that it spawns leads to a shifting and transient on-site labour force. This accounts for many of the problems of sustained union organising. Less than half of all construction workers are in unions. Such a work organisation is not only obstructive to the development of workers' organisation, but also makes even management control and supervision difficult. The incentive to work flat out is provided by an elaborate system of piecework and bonus payments. Most bonuses are related to output, and payment is according to work done. Despite trade union efforts, the basic wage in building remains low. "The bonus element is particularly important as it constitutes half of average earnings. In practice, basic rates are simply a guaranteed minimum earnings level."[13] The essence of the operation is speed of work. The employment of casual labour on high bonuses provides both the sub-contractors and the main contractors with the means for meeting targets and carving out surpluses from within agreed contracts. Since the inflation of the past decade, most contracts now contain clauses providing for fluctuations in prices, giving the contractor just a little more elbow room for manipulating operations.[14]

The contractor's ability to hire and fire workers for a "lump" sum is vital to operating the contracting system successfully. Since the Second World War, especially during the years of the building boom in the 1960s and early 1970s, this form of employment has grown.[15] In 1975 the Department of the Environment estimated that at least 220,000 building workers were directly working on the "Lump".[16] Exact figures are difficult to ascertain and in the past the numbers working in the industry have been underestimated by a quarter of a million or more. Such employment practices mean continual changes in the labour force in response to the changing requirements of individual developments and projects as they are worked through and to new sites when they are started. The experience of unemployment is common among building workers. Even in the final year of the building boom some 90,000 workers were unemployed. Five years later, in 1978, a quarter of a million building operatives were out of work, 14% of all unemployed.[17]

The employment of casual labour on such a scale has weakened the power of the trade unions, helped undermine the position of skilled trades, such as electricians, plumbers, carpenters, and plasterers, and struck a blow at apprenticeships. The labour force has undergone a process of de-skilling. Nowhere is this more apparent than in the reduction of the number of indentured apprentices during the height of the building boom, between 1964 and 1973, from 66,000 to 32,000.[18] Trades are diluted under cover of the

"Lump". Whereas other strongholds of such labour practices, most recently the docks, succumbed in this century to decasualisation, building has not. It depends on such labour and today, as always throughout its history as a capitalist enterprise, it is in the forefront in exploiting cheap immigrant labour—traditionally the Irish, but now also Asians and West Indians.

Whatever immediate benefits may accrue to individual workers in terms of non-payment of taxes and insurance contributions, these are far outweighed for building workers collectively by the insecurity of employment, low basic pay, lack of insurance cover and pension, and the inadequacy or absence of strong trade union protection. One of the most appalling consequences of such work organisation is the disregard for elementary safety and health precautions— hence the high rate of accidents and death in the industry, higher than any other. In 1975 40% of all industrial deaths were in construction: 181 building workers lost their lives. On the basis of present trends it is estimated that every other day a building worker will die. Under the present contract system workers are paid for the length of the trench, not the quality of the shoring, for the square of scaffolding, not the number and security of ties holding it back to the building or the inclusion of toeboards and guard rails. Thus, it is not surprising that James Tye, Director General of the British Safety Council, should state: "The significant thing about this accident [failure of riveter's staging which sent the worker in it 180 feet to his death], which would not be considered in a factory inspector's investigation, is that riveters are paid on this job by the hundred rivets, not for the time it takes them to put up the staging. Needless to say, they try to get the staging put up in the shortest possible time, so that they can start earning. Many accidents like this are caused not by the nature of the work, but by the speed at which the work is expected to be done. Overtime increases the period at risk in dangerous conditions."[19] An official report on health and safety in the construction industry in the year 1976 analysed 100 on-site deaths and concluded that only 12 were not "reasonably forseeable". It concluded that 70% of accidents were due to falls of either operatives or materials. "The men involved were construction workers going about their normal work, they were not working at the frontiers of technology, they were simply picked off one at a time."[20] Whereas other traditionally dangerous industries, such as mining and shipping, have made progress in recent years regarding safety, building has not.

Forms of finance

The contract joins two types of capital investment, industrial capital in the form of the building firm and loan capital in the form of the purchaser/investor. Through time the bearer of the loan capital has undergone considerable changes: from the industrialist, to the shop-keepers and others of the traditional petit bourgeoisie, to the local authority and private financial institutions of today. Throughout all these changes the general building firm has changed surprisingly little. Whether large or small they tend to be flexible in their operations and move easily between differing types of building and maintenance work. At one end of the spectrum the large companies are involved in building office blocks as well as modernising blocks of flats, while at the other end, the small family firm may be filling in a vacant site with a mews cottage or converting an old Victorian house into flats for the local authority. Today, as in the past, such work is usually performed under contract by the builder, although there is always some speculative building taking place, particularly in periods of boom for the industry, when the chances of finding a buyer in the open market are considered good. But whether speculative or to contract the level of activity in the industry is dependent on the availability of loan capital either through state expenditure or via the private institutions of finance capital. The daily operations of the building firm are financed through credit on materials and by overdraft or by borrowing from a merchant or fringe bank or by entering into partnership with a financial institution.

Most building firms, when not working to a contract, work in partnership with or in close association with a property company which is responsible for the financing of the project, whether it be a new building or a conversion.

Since the War the annual production of houses has fluctuated, quite widely, around the 300,000 mark. In most years private housing has accounted for over half the houses built. During the decade of the 1960s, of the 3½ million houses built close to 2 million were in the private sector. In other words, for every three council dwellings built there are four private ones.[21] In either case, private or council, the main source of monies invested is finance capital and it is the building societies, banks, insurance companies and pension funds that profit from the interest repayments.

Virtually all the new additions to the housing stock are built by private builders. Very little housing is built by local authorities' own labour, the direct labour force. In 1924, for example, they built slightly less than 10% of new local authority housing, around 8% in 1948, and only 5% in 1974.[22] Production of housing is overwhelmingly by private capital. Some of the larger builders invest in land with the aim of developing at the appropriate time of upswing in the property market. The Department of the Environment commissioned a study which gives some indication of the land holdings—land banks as they are termed—held by building companies. The report noted that the "bigger companies with land banks are able to report a substantial increase in profits in years of increased demand, holding a disproportionate share of the land . . . than their size within the industry in terms of numbers of houses built each year might justify". One of the largest such holdings was the 42,000 acres owned by Northern Developments.[23] In 1975, the year that the report was issued, the firm looked very successful; three years later it went into liquidation.[24]

Jerry-building

When it comes to quality in housing, the differences are as profound as the cleavages in class relations. When in 1913 the soap magnate, Sir Arthur Crosfield, had a 65-room mansion built atop Highgate West Hill, it was not only large but also soundly built and graciously styled and furnished in fine detail. It combined the skill of the building crafts with the best in materials. In 1976 it sold for £1,300,000. It is estimated that this spacious family home and garden costs the equivalent of a dozen school teachers' salaries to run.[25] When it comes to the provision of low cost housing to meet the needs of workers, haste and poor materials characterise both new building and the conversion, rehabilitation, of old. Jerry-building, meaning building hastily with bad materials, is as old as capitalist industry and the towns it spawned.

The outcome of private capital and the contracting system is jerry-built housing. The low level of labour productivity in house building is circumvented by substituting lower grade materials and labour than those contracted for and producing a finished product of poor quality. The examples are many and well documented. The newspaper *Building Design* printed in January 1979 the results of its survey into defects in recent local authority housing. After "the quick-build days of the 50s and 60s" the results of the private contractors' activities are all too clearly revealed: "rain penetration through flat roofs, defective windows, poorly installed or grossly expensive heating systems, spalling claddings and crumbling concrete panels. Rotting wall ties are a growing headache . . . "[26] Whether the dwellings were built according to traditional or, as in many cases, to new industrialised methods there is a general consistency in their having been shoddily built.

Right across the country local authorities are facing bills running into millions of pounds to rectify the low standard of construction. In Bootle, for example, repairs "costing £250,000 are being carried out on the 22-storey residential block, Strand House, built ten years ago as part of a shopping development. The block suffered shrinkage of its load-bearing concrete frame, causing spalling of concrete cladding . . . ", meaning that the concrete facings were becoming loose and chunks of it were liable to fall off. "Inspections revealed that expansion joints were not large enough. Improved joints are now being installed, and cladding replaced with brickwork. The builders were not held to blame 'given the extent of knowledge' at the time." Another example is Basingstoke: "The total cost of remedial work on five blocks of maisonettes . . . has now reached more than £300,000—as much as the 92 units cost to build in 1969." Many authorities— in London, the Midlands and in Wales and throughout the North—are having to demolish whole estates built since the last War. Just one example: in Newcastle, "Noble Street has been the scene of two demolitions by the city council since the war. In September 434 flats built by the city in 1955 to replace slum dwellings were demolished at a cost of £101,000".

The authors of the survey are not too sure of the explanation, but tend to point an accusing finger at politicians demanding too many housing starts and the ignorance of architects. However, the signed statement of a building operative given prominence in the report points a beam of light right through to the core of the contracting system and its organisation of work. The statement reads as follows:

"In situ re-inforcing steel was left out or simply thrown into slab joints without spacers.
Rarely was a poker used on in-situ concrete.
Concrete and dry-pack were shovel-batched, no control on cement or water content.
Damaged units were erected and later dressed to disguise uneven joints, etc. In at least three instances I saw damaged floor panels erected, including a completely cracked one.
Levelling bolts were cut off and wall panels levelled on hardboard shims.
Dry-pack placed by tamping with pieces of timber.
Retaining loops on staircase panels were cut off to make erection easy.

Parapet panels were delivered and erected green,
some so green that they fell to pieces when lifted.
Incorrect reinforcing was used on parapet panels.
Stiching joints were often not completely filled.
Wall units were erected out of plumb.
Face panels often cracked near windows, but were
used anyway."[27]

Bad materials, hastily used.

One of the most serious problems to arise in local
authority housing stock built since the Second World
War is dampness and mould growth. As yet no proper
investigation has been made to establish the extent of
the problem, although it is known to exist in hundreds
of thousands of dwellings up and down the country.
Many tenants have lived in such bad housing conditions for an entire generation or more with whole
rooms and built-in cupboards sometimes unusable. In
some cases the damp and the fungus is the direct
result of the design of the dwellings. There are
instances of pre-fabricated blocks of flats made of concrete slabs which act like stone cooling jars and where
the moisture from the air literally runs down the walls.
In other cases it results from a combination of skimping on the specified insulating materials, even leaving
them out altogether, and the use of cheap and inef-
fective forms of central heating. These conditions of
internal dampness can be injurious to health especially
where people already suffer from respiratory problems. Again it is the consequence of building quickly
and on the cheap in order to keep within the cost
restrictions imposed on local authority house-
building.[28]

The present crisis

The present crisis in capitalist production is bringing
about significant changes in industrial organisation
and location. It is a period in which capital is undergoing a process of restructuring. The position of the
larger firms is being consolidated and capital further
concentrated into fewer hands. Changes are also being
brought about in the organisation of the labour process

itself, reducing both the quantity and skill of labour employed. One such example is the steel industry, where basic changes in the labour process are being forced through. It is a general phenomenon throughout capitalist production, although not necessarily on the same scale as the case of steel production.

The building industry is currently under extreme pressure, both from within and from without, to cut back on the costs of new house building and conversions. From inside there is the pressure from the trade unions to bring about the decasualisation of the industry. The builders are divided between the National Federation of Building Trades Employers, which covers the larger companies and is prepared to contemplate some move towards decasualisation, and the Federation of Master Builders, made up of small jobbing concerns mostly employing non-union casual labour, and opposed to any such move. Genuine decasualisation would bring about enormous changes in the industry and spur rapid advances in the development and application of far more advanced industrialised building methods.

From outside the industry there is the interest of capital generally in cutting back the necessary costs of production. Housing is just such a cost, constituting an important part of the overall cost of reproducing labour power. Working class demands for improved housing standards increase the pressure for cutting the costs of its provision. In other similar areas of social need, such as health and education, state intervention has displaced the commodity form in order to meet these needs, however inadequately.

But here we come face to face with "a major contradiction within capitalism—between those who make profits from housing and those who want to minimise housing costs"[29]. Thomas Angotti, in pin-pointing the contradiction, explains it as arising between the bulk of capitalists wanting to minimise this cost and the investors in the construction and finance sectors who want to maximise it.[30] This contradiction and how it is balanced determines both the extent of public housing and the amount of direct public sector building and maintenance. The whole question of state policy and housing finance will be explored in the next chapter. But here a brief discussion is needed of public sector building in the form of the employment of direct labour by local authorities.

Local authority construction activity is both necessary under the conditions of capitalist production and at the same time is in potential rivalry with private capitals. Hence in the present period of recession in the industry a campaign is being waged against the whole principle of direct labour and the provision of more public sector work to private contractors is demanded.

Direct labour

Local authorities do a great deal of building. In 1973, their new construction work alone in England and Wales was valued at £2,200 million—over a quarter of total construction output. The largest single item was new housing. Adding repair and maintenance, local authority work represents well over a third of total construction output.[31] But most of this work is farmed out to private contractors, and the local authorities' own labour forces are responsible for about a third, mostly maintenance work rather than new building.

In principle, direct labour represents a real alternative to private contracting: a permanent labour force, with guaranteed wage, insurance cover and pension, a planned and continuous work-load, publicly accountable and responsive to tenants' needs. In reality, direct labour suffers from under-equipment, low wage rates and low bonus payments compared to the private sector. It is very much the poor cousin of the building industry and its finances are strictly controlled. In this sense it cannot compete with the "Lump" when it comes to actual earnings. Given that most of its work is general repairs and little actual new building, the employment of skilled trades and apprenticeship schemes suffer. Often direct labour covers the work private contractors will not touch. In a period of cuts in public expenditure, such as the present, the council employee is often blamed for the problems of poor building standards and lack of repairs common to most council housing. Despite these conditions of subordination to the interests of private contractors some direct labour departments, such as Manchester's, have achieved a reputation for high standard and efficient work. But generally direct labour suffers from poor pay and morale, petty corruption, and a management favouring private contracting and without any commitment to developing a building and repair service responsive to tenants' needs. In this situation the workers, although organised, remain on the defensive.

Like education and health, state expenditure on housing is being cut back. New housing starts are at their lowest for thirty years. The amount being spent on conversion and up-grading of existing old stock is reduced. The numbers employed in the direct labour forces throughout the country are falling from the peak of 200,000 achieved in the 1960s. Although this is an area of social expenditure vital to the social reproduction of capitalism, cuts are imposed not simply to boost profits in the private sector but also in order to help facilitate both the restructuring of capital, in terms of shifts in places of employment and the types of labour employed, and the restructuring of these services themselves. Hence the new medical technologies located in large regional hospitals, the closure of schools and the move to larger units and new educational technologies, and housing—new forms of rent payment, shifting repairs (minor) and decorations on to the tenant, and new systems of security (entrance-phone). If the housing shortage begins to pinch it must be remembered that housing is a necessary institution in the location and formation of the labour force.

Chapter 4
Housing policy

Political intervention

With the passing of the Increase of Rent and Mortgage Interest (War Restrictions) Act of 1915, the immediate price of housing, whether in the form of weekly or monthly rent or mortgage payments, was rendered a political question and became subject to regulation by the state. This political intervention into the housing market was considered a temporary expedient that would end with the overcoming of the housing shortage. The regulation of rent levels and interest rates was followed in the early 1920s by other measures designed to stimulate, by various subsidies, the building of houses for sale or rent. In the early 1930s building societies and mortgagees were given further tax relief to encourage investment in housing. These interventions by the state into the financing of housing in turn created the need for further legislation affecting the landlord-tenant relation. The security of occupancy of differing categories—furnished and unfurnished—of tenants in the private sector required changing in order to stop controls being circumvented by summary evictions.

The existence of these measures affecting rent and interest levels, the payment of subsidies, and changes in the law governing landlord-tenant relations, taken together represented a new balance in "the generalised class struggle over items of consumption".[1] With the formation of the Labour Party at the beginning of the century the working class came to intervene directly in the bargaining process of parliamentary politics. As a consequence, the strategy of the state towards housing became a series of measures aimed at accommodating the demand for improvements in housing while preserving the conditions of their profitable production and provision. Between 1918 and 1939, the years of peace, nearly all the 4 million or so houses built, even for local authorities, were the work of private contractors and roughly three out of every four were sold privately.[2]

The state was extending its intervention in a period of crisis for capitalism, as it moved from the phase of small-scale competitive capitals to that of monopoly capital dominant today. In the process the whole framework of political debate and policy-making changed. The assumptions and parameters of laissez-faire thinking were gradually displaced by notions of public responsibility and involvement in social matters. The Labour Party helped in the creation of this new framework for political debate and policy formation with its ideology of the welfare state. The Labour Party as a reformist party sought to represent through the electoral bargaining process the immediate interests of the working class: their interests as wage-earners. The history of the Labour Party, and of social democracy generally, is not that of the politically innocent being ensnared by the cunning of bourgeois parliamentary politics: on the contrary, the Party is an essential part of those politics. The Labour Party participated in creating the political framework, the politics of welfare, through which the accommodation of the class struggle takes place. Parliamentary politics—its periodic elections, party programmes, legislative procedures and enactments—is a process of bargaining through which the political conditions are reproduced for the continuing accommodation and collaboration of classes.

Policy in an area such as housing is never simply the imposition and carrying out of one party's programme in the direct, even if immediate, interests of a particular class or fraction of a class, but is itself a product of the bargaining process as established in the modern representative state of capitalist society. Actual policy is always subject to the state's practice of upholding the general conditions of capitalist production and the dominance of the capitalist class as a whole. So from the outset the political intervention into the housing market involved successive Governments—eventually Labour ones too—in the contradiction of protecting the immediate interests of tenants while preserving the dominant interests of private capital in the building and ownership of housing. The contradiction has been most acute in the case of the private rented sector. It has been subject to the decline of the rentier petit bourgeoisie, which was gradually displaced by the institutions of finance capital as they came to play an ever more important role in the 20th century in the ownership and development of urban land and property. At the level of policy-making, the decline in the private landlord was not recognised as a consequence of the more general change in structure of capitalist production but as the result of state intervention itself. The effect had the appearance of a cause, so housing policy has involved continuous changes in the degree and extent of rent regulation, interest rates and tax relief, and the legal provisions for ending tenancies. Party positions in housing have been formed within the framework of perceivable immediate needs of given social classes and groups and the possibilities of state involvement. The dividing line that came to distinguish Conservative and Labour policy on housing from the 1920s through to the beginning of the 1960s was their respective commitment to either the market or the state as the principal regulator in housing provision and allocation. It was never a question of either private or social ownership of the housing stock but a matter of weighting and the part to be played by each.

Ever since the first legislative measures controlling rents, successive Conservative and Labour Governments have attempted to alter the balance between the private and public sectors, first one way and then the other. Ironically it was the last of the Liberal Governments that broke with its laissez-faire ideas on housing to give local authorities subsidies to encourage them to build dwellings for rent. The two inter-war Labour Governments, formed in 1924 and 1929, took measures to encourage house building and slum clearance by providing subsidies to local authorities and private builders. The various Conservative Governments of the inter-war period tended to pass measures cutting the level of subsidy, reducing the restrictions on rent levels in both the private and public sectors and generally weakening the security of private tenancies and shifting the balance in favour of the landlord. Indeed, in the 1930s they went a long way in eroding the state's role in housing until the outbreak of War in 1939 brought about the re-imposition of controls, once again conceived as a temporary expedient.

For twenty years following World War II the battle lines between Conservatives and Labour were much as before. In the face of the continuing decline of the private landlord, the disrepair and overcrowding of much of the privately rented stock, the two parties restated their solutions to the housing problem. The Conservative position was summed up in the Government's White Paper of 1953, *Houses—the Next Step*.[3] Housing needs were to be met principally through the market, the century-long decline of private landlordism was to be stopped and owner-occupation encouraged as a vital ingredient of a property-owning democracy. In opposition the Labour Party issued its own declaration of intent, *Homes for the Future*.[4] The commitment was to take profits out of housing provision and make it a social service by gradually extending public ownership to the greater part of the housing stock and leaving owner-occupation to the middle and upper classes. Forms of ownership and tenure were at stake rather than the financing and production of housing.

While in office from 1945 to 1951, Labour continued war-time controls over rents and building and made available low-interest loans to local authorities in an effort to overcome the immediate shortages causing overcrowding and homelessness and giving rise to agitation and direct action from returning soldiers and their families. After the Conservative's election victory in 1951, the Government removed controls on building and set into motion the process of slowly decontrolling rents in the private sector. The Housing Repairs Act, 1954, and the notorious Rent Act of 1957 opened the way to the decontrolling and raising of rents.[5] The hope was to stop the decline in the private rented sector, but it had the opposite effect, with widespread speculation in the housing market and the removal of tenants, by fair means and foul, so as to sell with vacant possession. The old habit of winkling out tenants against both their wishes and legal rights acquired a new name from one of those actively and profitably engaged in the practice at the time, Perec Rachman. The private landlord continued to take leave from the housing market. Between 1957 and 1965 the number of private dwellings for renting fell by some 2 million.[6] Private interests promoted the decline in the privately rented sector—a fact that politicians of both major parties were slow in understanding. At the same time the role of the local authorities in the provision of housing for the working class was reduced and in 1959 the Housing Purchase and Housing Act was passed to stimulate individual home ownership.

The return of a Labour Government in 1964 revealed for the first time the two principal political parties converging on the housing question. The Conservatives' emphasis on owner-occupation and the determination of rents by market forces was now informing Labour Government policy too. As early as 1961 Labour omitted its pledge on municipal housing from its policy statement, *Signposts for the Sixties*.[7] What this meant in practice became clear in 1965, when the Labour Government's Rent Act introduced the "fair rent" principle for determining the rent of unfurnished private tenants. The aim was to establish a new system of rent regulation for unfurnished accommodation. Rent officers and Rent Assessment Committees were given the task of setting rents offering reasonable returns—just a little profit—to the landlord. There was a back-up scheme of rent allowances to help poorer tenants willing to undergo a means test to meet the new regulated rents. In practice the landlord rather than the tenant benefited from the new machinery. Rent assessment panels generally raised rents and it was the landlord rather than the tenant who made use of them. An analysis of some 101,000 cases brought before these panels revealed that twice as many ended up being raised as were reduced. In 1970, 94% of all landlords who applied for an increase in rent were successful. Among the landlords it tended to be the bigger ones and the expanding property companies that benefited most from registering rents in this way.[8]

The division between Labour and Conservative policy became less and less distinct. In 1972 a Conservative Government extended the "fair rent" principle throughout the private sector to include the remaining enclave of controlled tenants in the older housing stock of low rateable value, and included for the first time the public sector. The aim was to achieve "a regulated free market rent" throughout all rented accommodation. The long-run objective was to achieve a degree of comparability and market accountability to housing allocation as a whole. The hope was to reduce substantially the amount of central government subsidies going to public housing: £300 million was the figure set by the Government. To offset the obvious hardship the subsequent rise in rents would cause many households, a national rent rebate scheme was introduced for council tenants.

Although the Labour Party nationally was no longer committed to state provision of housing to meet general working class needs, and had supported the voluntary-run housing association movement as an alternative, such a commitment to social provision and ownership of housing was still strongly held in many areas of local Labour dominance. It was in the traditional Labour strongholds with a long tradition of municipalised housing that resistance to the Conservative Housing Finance Act of 1972 was strongest. It was in areas such as St. Pancras, now part of the London Borough of Camden, Clay Cross in the Midlands, Merthyr in South Wales and Clydebank and Saltcoats in Scotland, where active opposition not only to the Act but also to its actual implementation went furthest. The tradition of municipal socialism had hardy roots. There were well organised local campaigns. It was here that the local Councils held out longest against implementing the provisions of the Act, and when the rent increases were imposed the tenants organised a campaign of withholding payment. Such action gave strength to the national campaign and helped in the return of a Labour Government in 1974. The new Government froze rents for a year, provided a loan to the building societies in order to stop a further rise in mortgage rates and repealed those clauses in the 1972 Act which imposed "fair rents" on council dwellings. But as its later proposals in 1978 revealed, social ownership of housing was no longer taken to be the answer for meeting general housing needs.

Labour's retreat on the housing question was part of a more general abandonment of positions regarding the extent and nature of state provision in economic and social life. In the face of Western capitalism's deepest crisis since the 1930s, far-ranging cuts were made in public expenditure not only in housing but throughout both state-run industry and services and health, education and social welfare generally. The present situation has brought into question in a most practical way the idea of advancing to socialism through the accumulative effects of piecemeal reforms. The achievements of Social Democracy are being cut back in the interests of private capital and private profit. Again it is piecemeal—this time in reverse.

The need now is to look at the underlying realities upon which the policies of both parties foundered, for the housing question—rising rents, dilapidated and empty property, overcrowding and homelessness— still exists and is again a source of tension in social life in the current period of economic stagnation and high unemployment.

Alternative tenures

Although Labour have now largely abandoned their commitment to municipalisation as the solution to the housing problem, the question at the centre of state policy remains that of the weight to be given to each of the two major tenures: council and owner-occupation. This becomes a matter of growing importance in the present period of general cuts in public expenditure when the priority for capital, capitalist production as a whole, is to expand the amount of unpaid labour under its command. The struggle is primarily being fought out over changes in the labour process, deskilling, and a reduction in living standards for workers through wage restraint and cuts in social expenditure. Clearly in the case of working class housing any rise in rents or mortgage rates will cut into wages. Living standards will fall either because of the increase in payments for housing or because in the face of higher rents and interest payments people are forced to take accommodation of a lower standard or must share in overcrowded circumstances or become homeless—all of which does happen.

In the inter-party debates of parliamentary politics, argument rages over the extent to which the two major tenures involve public monies from either rates or taxes or from both. The council tenant is seen as being subsidised at the expense of the rate payer in particular, while the owner-occupier is subsidised in the form of tax relief on mortgage repayments. These arguments can enter into matters of extreme complexity when trying to assess the various costs of services such as roads and sewers, management and maintenance costs, the costs of professional services of surveyors and valuers, as well as the land and building costs and the general costs of loan charges. Who, then, is the most subsidised? And who is getting the best deal financially? The one tenure is pitted against the other. As long as the question is approached from the standpoint of the individual it is very much a matter of chance and circumstance as to which tenure is the most advantageous. Did the person become an owner-occupier when house prices were low? Is the household small or large? Is the council tenant living in an old property with a relatively low rent? In any case is the income of the household, whether a lone individual or a family, stable and secure, high or low? Clearly individual circumstances of income and family size can distinguish any two households with the same tenure whether it be council or mortgagee.

What these arguments fail to recognise is that the subsidies, whether out of the rates or from central government, or in the form of tax relief, are not subsidies to individual households at all. This is merely their appearance, the immediate form of their presentation as financial advantage to the individual mortgagee or rent payer. In reality, these subsidies are "explicitly designed to finance" a part of the interest charges, the cost of finance, "imposed by loan charges"[9]. In short, these subsidies are transfers of public money to finance capital.

If we compare the two tenures in relation to the housing needs of the working class the general advantage of the council tenure is obvious. In the private market for housing the value of dwellings is determined by the newly built properties entering the market, which places individual purchase outside the range of most workers. The much vaunted capital gain to be made by transferring from one house to another, while of advantage to the well-off, inflates house prices out of all proportion to prices generally. In the 30 years since the war (until the end of 1977), whereas retail prices increased 6½ times, house values increased 10 times and industrial share values only less than 5 times.[10]

The situation with council housing is different. Ever since the Housing Revenue Account was introduced by statute in 1935, local authorities have been able to pool their rents. The housing stock of most local authorities consists of dwellings built or acquired at various times and their costs to the council will vary accordingly. The original or "historic" costs of an estate built in the 1920s or 1930s is but a fraction of the costs of a housing project built today. Past investments are held at their fixed historic costs. It is only with new investment that the debt increases.[11] A local authority can spread the rents it charges over the whole of its stock and does not have to fix them in direct relation to the actual costs of particular dwellings. It is this pooling of rents that makes it possible for local authorities to build housing for working class households to live in. If there was no such pooling and rents had to be directly related to the costs of construction, state subsidies alone would not suffice in keeping rent levels within the financial means of workers. At present the high costs of new council dwellings are shared by all the tenants. This pooling of rents is not so much a case of tenants subsidising each other as a matter of together sharing in the burden of the loan charges and building costs imposed on local authority housing.[12]

The pooling of rents gives council housing a definite economic advantage over other tenures, including the declining private rented sector, when it comes to providing for working class housing needs. There are other advantages, despite the inefficiency and authoritarianism characteristic of state bureaucracy. Allocation of dwellings to households, for example, can be much more rational in the public sector, with the size of households, age and particular disabilities being taken into account. Given the fact that owner-occupation cannot be a tenure general to the working class, as the price of such housing requires a level and regularity of income uncharacteristic of most, although not all, categories of working class employment, the council tenure cannot be done away with. It may be cut back in size a little and the standard of repair and management allowed to decline, as in the present period of economic stagnation and cuts in social expenditure. Indeed there is a distinct advantage even to a capitalist state in the existence of council housing, in that it not only offers a partial solution to meeting the housing needs of the working class but also allows for the comprehensive redevelopment of those parts of the housing stock that either through age or neglect fall into decay and need replacing.

Owner-occupation, however, is of definite advantage to capital as a whole and not just to the financial institutions directly profiting from it. Home ownership underpins "the whole structure of consumer credit . . ."[13] "Sales of consumer durables, frequently made on credit, are more often than not secured against freehold ownership: thus the manufacturers, importers and retailers of cars, freezers, washing machines, colour television sets, sound systems, furniture, garden accessories and so on in their turn rely on the appreciating value of houses to maintain the demand for their product."[14] For a specific fraction of capital, represented above all by the building societies, this tenure has the advantage that unlike council housing, the indebtedness increases merely by virtue of people buying and reselling houses and taking out fresh mort-gages. There need not even be any new dwellings constructed for this revaluation process to take place. This is quite the opposite to the council tenure where the debt only increases with new investment.[15] Hence owner-occupation will always be the dominant tenure.

Some financial institutions, such as banks and insur-ance companies, encourage individual home owner-ship amongst the better paid and qualified sections of their employees. The National Westminster Bank aids 58.6% of its 48,300 labour force with mortgages, pur-chasing advice, rent allowances, and beds in company hostels and flats; the Prudential Assurance Company assists 49% of its 21,365 employees with a house-pur-chase scheme.[16] For the company there is the double advantage of interest payments and a stabilizing effect on specialized segments of the workforce.

The advantages of this tenure for capital are not merely a matter of cash but are also of immense ideological importance. Home ownership helps underpin and leg-itimise the possession of private property so dear to the heart of every capitalist. Owning one's own home is held up as the ideal to which all should aspire if not actually subscribe. For the worker, owner-occupation can prove a burden. There is the ever-present fear of falling behind with the mortgage payments, court orders, and the possible repossession of the dwelling by the lender. A study of 400 council mortgages in Birmingham showed 32 to have failed and a further 31 at risk mostly for being more than six months in arrears. Repossession may leave people in debt as well as homeless. For instance, one owner, a labourer employed by the local authority, who had bought his house for £1,950 with a £1,650 mortgage in 1965, was repossessed for arrears four years later. The house was sold by the council for £850, leaving him still £1,189 in debt.[17] Even when these payments are met regularly and with little difficulty, there are problems of repairs and improvements which are often beyond the means of the household, especially when they are pension-ers. There is no guarantee against squalor and decay of the dwelling in this tenure. Most damaging of all, the worker is isolated and finds it extremely difficult to protest, let along fight back, against rising repair costs and interest repayments. As an investment it is one that can only be realized on leaving the tenure, which for most people will be when they die.

The problems that can face working class owner-occupiers are highlighted by the experience of many immigrant workers. There is a much higher level of owner-occupation amongst working class Asians and West Indians than white workers, largely because of the residency requirements applying to most local authority lettings. For many immigrants, buying has proved the only way of acquiring accommodation of anywhere near adequate size and cost. Four out of five Asian workers are owner-occupiers. Generally immigrants buy the cheaper, often sub-standard property, in the same decaying neighbourhoods that they first moved into on arrival in this country. Recent surveys show that the houses tend to be in poor repair, often lacking in the basic amenities of a bath, hot water and inside lavatory, and often involve households sharing. A detailed survey of immigrant housing conditions concluded:

"There are many Asian and West Indian owner-occupiers who might improve the quality of housing by moving into a council house, if they could get one, even though they would be likely to get sub-standard council housing. *Good* council housing would probably be an improvement on their accommodation for a majority of Asian and West Indian owner-occupiers."[18]

But owner-occupation usually excludes people, whatever their class or race, from the allocation systems used by local authorities.

Public subsidies

Both of the main tenures, council and owner-occupation, are supported by public subsidies. These subsidies fall into three main categories: general subsidies paid to local authorities giving substantial support to their provision of housing, subsidies in the form of tax relief to support mortgage payments, and, lastly, income-related rent rebates and rent allowances. All these subsidies have grown enormously in recent years and pose a growing problem to governments, whether Labour or Conservative, in the present period of financial stringency in public expenditure.

The general subsidies paid to local authorities are the best known, the more detailed and the most widely discussed and debated of all such expenditures. These subsidies are mostly from central government although there is some local contribution from the rates. For the financial year 1978/79 these general subsidies amount to £1,440 million, including £245 million in contribution from the local rates.[19] Basically these payments of public monies make up the difference in the local authority housing accounts, known as the Housing Revenue Account, between the income received in rents and the costs involved in financing, maintaining and managing the housing stock. These subsidies, which have more than doubled in amount during the 1970s, meet about half of the local authorities' total expenses on housing, the rest being met from rents. Two-thirds of the total outgoings of the Housing Revenue Account, for 1978/79, are repayment of the loans undertaken to build or acquire the houses in the first place. The remaining third of expenditure is to cover the costs of repairs and management. These figures are averages for the whole of England and Wales and conceal both considerable variations and changes in some urban areas. In London the early 1970s saw local authorities acquiring a lot of the older privately rented housing stock which greatly increased their indebtedness. The inner London Borough of Camden, for example, in 1971/2 spent £8¼ million on its housing account and required about £4¼ million in subsidies from central government and the rates in order to balance the books. Five years later its total expenditure amounted to £35¼ million requiring almost £25¼ million in subsidies to balance the accounts.[20]

Why is it that as local authorities acquire more and more "capital assets" in the form of housing they sink deeper and deeper into debt? The crucial feature about local authority house building and acquisition is that it is not self-financing but is almost entirely based on loans. In general the funds necessary for enlarging the housing stock are borrowed either directly from the capital market or through the Public Works Loan Board which acts as an intermediary between private loan capital and the local authorities. The expansion of the public sector in housing has thus meant growing indebtedness and dependency on private financial institutions. By the 1970s more than two-thirds of all local authority expenditure on housing was in interest charges on money borrowed. Take the example of Camden again: in 1978 its outstanding capital debt for housing stood at £298 million, a debt averaging out at £1,700 per man, woman and child living in the borough. The annual charges on this debt amount to £22½ million, 64 per cent of the Borough's expenditure on its housing account.[21] For England and Wales as a whole the recent period of expansion in local authority housing saw a tripling of the total housing debt so that by 1973/4 it stood at £11,500 million with annual loan charges close to £650 million.[22] What happens is that every time a local authority builds a new dwelling, costing perhaps in the mid-1970s around £10,000, it must borrow the money to finance the project and normally pays off the loan over a 60-year period. If the interest rate is 8 per cent then the ultimate cost of the dwelling will be £60,000: land, materials and labour £10,000, interest on the money borrowed to finance the project £50,000. This in a nutshell is the reason for the enormous debt and loan charges burdening local authority housing and the need for large general subsidies from central government to cover them.

Subsidies to the other major tenure, owner-occupation, are comparable in size. The estimate for 1978/9 is £1,265 million, slightly down on the previous year. This is because tax relief is even more sensitive to change in interest rates than general subsidies to public housing, because there is no dampening effect of pooling loans, for different periods of time. In addition to tax relief on mortgage repayments there is also the possible gain to be made, untaxed, when selling a house and buying another. It is estimated that in 1979 the amount of capital gains tax foregone in house trading amounted to £1,500 million—"larger than mortgage tax relief".[23]

The building societies dominate this tenure. They are financial institutions rivalling the banks both in total assets and as depositories for savings. In 1977 their total membership, shareholders and borrowers combined, embraced nearly 20 million persons. The value of their total assets exceeded £30,000 million.[24] The volume of tax relief is largely determined, apart from the tax rate itself, by the total volume of mortgage debt. This trebled in size in the eight years between 1969 and 1977.[25] This is a debt that will grow along with the revaluation process of the existing stock. The growth in this tenure and the continuing rise in house prices, even if interest rates remains fairly steady, will result in the growth of this subsidy in the form of tax relief.

The owner-occupation tenure is primarily a middle and upper-middle class tenure. The average income of first time buyers in 1975 was £3,753, compared with the average earnings of £3,161 for all male workers, and £2,896 for manual workers. Additionally, the average mortgage loan was £7,292 on a £9,549 property; thus the average deposit a first-time buyer had to find was £2,257. Two-thirds of first-time buyers paid less than this: nevertheless, only 11 per cent paid less than £500, and only 38 per cent less than £1,000. The majority of people taking out mortgages (53 per cent) were not first-time buyers but were merely changing homes, and the average income of these buyers was £4,299. The full breakdown for mortgages by annual income of borrowers in 1975 is as follows:

Income	Percentage of mortgages granted
under £2,000	3
£2,000–£2,999	24
£3,000–£3,999	32
£4,000–£4,999	20
over £5,000	21

Thus, only about 27 per cent of borrowers were earning under average earnings for 1975.[26] In this tenure the higher a person's income and the higher the initial purchase price of the dwelling the greater the tax relief. Also it is the better paid, especially those engaged in middle class careers and in receipt of regular incremental rises in income, who are in a position to make money out of selling their house or flat and buying another.

Finally, there are the income-related subsidies, means tested, paid on application to individuals with low incomes to help not only with rents but also with mortgage interest payments such as when an owner-occupier is on supplementary benefit. In 1978/9 the Supplementary Benefit Commission paid out £700 million pounds, mostly towards rent payments, including the private sector. Rent rebates in the council sector amounted in total to £500 million during the same financial year. Rent rebates are an actual reduction in the rent paid by the amount of the rebate, whereas rent allowances are in the form of cash payments to assist with the rent. Unlike the other subsidies these are "all transfer payments which redistribute income to individuals without directly paying for goods and services . . ."[27], whereas the other two subsidies are not really payments to individuals at all but are transfers of public money to finance capital.

Expenditure cuts

The Welfare State, however beneficial to capital and its rule, is not simply a device for the successful reproduction of capitalism but is a product of class struggle and represents the political basis of continuing class collaboration. In a period such as the present, state expenditure, which is in effect a transfer of value from the unpaid labour under capital's command, is a burden to capital, and unchecked welfare activities can hinder the much-needed redeployment of labour. The problem facing the state's housing policy is the size and growth in subsidies. The subsidy attacked is the one most immediately advantageous to the working class: the general subsidy to the local authority Housing Revenue Account. From the Labour Government of 1964 onwards it was clear that the principle of universality in the provision of council housing had been abandoned and that subsidies would be selective and not open-ended.

The Conservatives' Housing Finance Act of 1972 focused attention on the growth in the public sector subsidy and devised a policy for reducing its expected future growth by some £300 million. The aim of the Act was first to stabilise the subsidy going to public sector housing and eventually do away with it altogether. In order to achieve this, the annual rent income on local authority housing was to increase towards the point at which it equalled the total annual expenditure on debt repayment, repairs and management. It was envisaged that some authorities might make a surplus and others, facing large housing problems, a deficit which would be met partly by the Exchequer and partly from the rates. In order to achieve this virtual elimination of the general subsidy the local authorities lost their freedom to determine their own rent levels and the "fair rent" formula devised by the Labour government for the private sector was extended to council housing as well. The rent for a council dwelling was to be fixed according to private market criteria and irrespective of its costs. Control over rents passed from local authorities to rent scrutiny boards appointed by the government. The Secretary of State for the Environment was given the statutory powers to stop all subsidies and place the housing powers of an unco-operative local authority in the hands of a housing commissioner directly responsible to central government. A doubling in rent levels was expected. The increase would be phased and a complicated means-tested system of rent rebates was introduced to offset some of the hardship that would follow from the rises. The cost of the rebate scheme was to be spread amongst council tenants as a whole. Similar rent increases were to take place in the unfurnished private sector and a rent allowance scheme would help those in need. Financing people, not buildings, was the way Conservative politicians spoke of the new Act.

It was an Act designed to stop the growth in the council tenure, work towards the elimination of the general subsidy and structure rents so as to maximise payment in relation to incomes. New council building was no longer to be based on the fixed subsidies that had existed from 1923 to 1972. Such subsidies would be earmarked and selectively applied. The other side of the policy was the further encouragement of the other major tenure, owner-occupation, supplemented later, at the end of the 1960s, by a policy of encouraging the sale of individual council dwellings.

The new arrangements were never allowed to fully work themselves through. The return of a Labour Government in 1974 brought a temporary freeze on rents and the repeal of those sections of the Act imposing "fair" or market rents on council housing. It too had to face the problem of state expenditure on housing and ways of limiting the further growth in subsidies. The then Labour Secretary of State for the Environment, Anthony Crosland, on taking office in 1974 undertook a review of housing policy intended to be "fundamental". The result was the Green Paper, *Housing Policy: A Conservative Document*, produced in 1977. Labour's own Housing Bill was to follow in 1979 but the general election intervened.

The Green Paper, like similar Government studies before it, saw the solution to the housing problem as just around the corner. It essentially depended on the building of enough new dwellings where they were needed. Subsidies for new building would be selective, in line with Conservative policy. The massive slum clearance and rebuilding programmes, involving the construction of some 220,000 houses in the new towns of England and Wales, important in the 1950s and 1960s, were seen as no longer appropriate and in need of replacement by a much more selective programme of inner-city rehabilitation of existing dwellings and much smaller new housing projects.

Although the Green Paper recognised that the Government could only indirectly affect house building for private sale, unlike local authority building, which is "primarily a matter for Government decision . . ."[28], it sought to encourage the "trend towards home ownership, which gives many people the kind of home they want. It reduces the demands made on the public sector. It helps with problems of mobility, particularly for people who need to move to a new area when changing jobs"[29]. With this in view the Government was "not opposed to the sales of council homes provided that they can be made without impairing an authority's ability to deal with pressing housing needs or to maintain a housing stock of adequate quality for renting".[30] Also the Government (Labour) was anxious to maintain the growth of housing associations fostered by its 1974 Housing Act which established the Housing Corporation to channel in public funds and oversee their expansion. At the end of the 70s housing associations were averaging 20,000 newly built units and 15,000 rehabilitated units. Housing associations are a form of private corporate landlord, established by a self-appointed committee, and dependent on public funds either from the local authority or from the Housing Corporation. For the Labour Government they represented an effective alternative to municipalisation in the face of the continuing decline of the traditional private rented sector.

The general subsidies to the two main tenures were to remain. The Report claimed that the differences in the two tenures were such that at best it could only be hoped that the financial assistance given by the state to the two major tenures was "broadly fair"[3]. The general subsidy to the public sector would be made more selective and would be related to the local rent and rate contribution. Also it was proposed to keep council rents rising in general line with earnings and restrict the income-related subsidy. The defeat of Labour in the general election of May 1979 saw the end of their proposed Housing Bill based upon this policy review.

Both major parties are confident that a solution to the housing problem can be worked out and that it can be achieved in a few years. The basic reason for this is the existence of a surplus of dwellings to households.

The estimates of this surplus, its size and quality, vary but it is likely that it amounts to about ½ million dwellings. This figure is a national average, so whether the dwellings are where households can live or of a price they can afford or even available for habitation are matters affecting the significance for housing policy of the existence of this crude surplus. In London, for example, the Borough of Westminster has the highest amount of empty dwellings, 13.8 per cent, and it stands next to the Borough of Brent which has the highest shortage of dwellings, an estimated deficit of 2.5 per cent.[32] But despite the proximity, the realities of social class means that the families and individuals in need of new homes living in Brent will not be able to cross the Borough boundary to gain access to the expensive vacant dwellings in Westminster.

Although the post-war years have seen an improvement in the overall basic standards of the housing stock with a reduction in the number of unfit dwellings and those lacking the basic amenities, the number in need of substantial repairs has risen during the past decade. Estimates put the number of homes requiring repairs of £1,000 or more at over 1 million dwellings and the total appears to be increasing.

Further, there is the problem that the housing stock is in constant need of renewal and refurbishing. Dwellings must be upgraded from time to time and replaced. Changes in the siting of production can render residential accommodation superfluous. Consequently there must be a continuing production of new dwellings and improvement of existing properties. Yet the number of houses started in the public sector in 1978 was 107,500—the lowest figure since World War II.[33] The private construction of dwellings is also down. House building is in a slump. The Government's expenditure plans for the early 1980s show the continuing effects of expenditure cuts in housing investment. The future expenditure on new housing is planned to remain at the new low level. The only real growth is expected to occur in the private construction of housing for owner-occupation.

But it is precisely in these moments when a solution to the housing problem seems possible that the realities of capitalist social relations assert themselves. Capital in its struggle to enlarge its share of the social wealth produced imposes restrictions on state expenditures. The subsidies going to housing are thus under review and are subject to new restrictions. The high returns to finance capital are not attacked, nor are the high costs of house building under the present contracting system, but instead the tenure of most advantage to the working class is to be trimmed and the financial burden to the tenants increased.

The class character of the distribution of accommodation means that even with an excess of dwellings people will be sharing, living in over-crowded conditions and subject to homelessness. Indeed, the "shortage" is a necessary mechanism in the deployment and disciplining of labour. In the present period of capitalism's difficulties and the restructuring of industry, the housing problem is likely to grow not lessen, with the result that whichever of the two major parties is the Government, housing policy will reflect the constraining realities of capitalist society. The options for shifting the balance between the two major tenures decline with the demise of the private landlord. Housing policy will increasingly concern itself over the forms and effectiveness of the financial support given to the two principal tenures of council and owner-occupation. The question of meeting the social need for accommodation will be buried under the welter of conflicting arguments over the benefits of home ownership and the rate-payers' support of council tenants.

Chapter 5
Gentrification: a case study

Displacing the working class

Gentrification is the name given to the process by which the original working class inhabitants of an area are displaced and the whole social character of a neighbourhood changed. The "gentry" are members of the middle classes: professional and managerial people. The area of housing may or may not originally have been intended for working class occupation. It may include a street of two-storey artisans' cottages or perhaps a mews of what were once servants quarters above stables, or again it can be streets of large Victorian houses which in some earlier period underwent the reverse change. This changing or turning-over of an area is nothing new but has happened again and again and is an integral part of capitalist urban development. In the past it was usually associated with slum clearance, with the poor being crowded into neighbouring streets and the new housing being acquired by members of the wealthier middle classes.

In the more recent past, especially in the 1960s and early 1970s when the property boom was at its height, this process of displacement took on a more subtle form. In a number of areas of Inner London the existing housing was not pulled down but its fabric repaired and modern facilities installed, while the former inhabitants made their homes elsewhere. The 1957 Rent Act, although meant to revive the private landlord, by de-controlling rents opened the way for the emptying of multi-occupied dwellings and their being put up for sale with vacant possession. It is a slow process. Individual houses, often suffering from years of neglect, became vacant one at a time. Some tenants are easily persuaded to move, others will only do so if offered comparable accommodation elsewhere, and still others are stubborn and want to stay in their homes. In the latter cases some tenants find themselves "sold" as sitting tenants in a property otherwise empty and suitable for conversion into a family home. Many others, with neighbours gone, find themselves harassed and in danger of being "winkled" out by their landlord or his agent. In the streets of Victorian terraced housing common to districts of Inner London this process was well underway by the end of the 1960s.

In 1969 a Housing Act was passed to facilitate the modernisation and upgrading of the housing stock. It was precisely these areas of multi-occupied, privately rented housing that were meant to benefit. Local authorities were given the power to make at their own discretion improvement grants of up to £1,200 tax free per dwelling. They could also declare entire districts "General Improvement Areas" and spend money on upgrading the general environment by closing streets, landscaping and planting trees. The grants for improving the housing, far from benefiting the tenant, more often than not were used to rehabilitate property that was empty in readiness for selling. In the main, improvement grants were little more than a disguised subsidy to property speculators successful in emptying houses. A striking example of the profit in such dealings was provided by a house in Camden. The property was bought by a developer in October 1971 for £12,000. Some £20,000 was spent on its conversion into a number of small self-contained flats for sale. For this the developer received improvement grants from the local authority totalling £9,640. The flats were put on the market at £12,500 for a one-bedroom unit and £14,750 for a two bedroom one. The expected profit for the developer from this whole operation of converting an old property was not far short of £90,000.

Both the 1957 and 1969 Acts, contrary to their intention, reinforced the decline in the private rented sector and the process of working class displacement. The change-over of a neighbourhood, known as gentrification, was speeded-up.

Housing in London – the context

The neighbourhood of this study is located within Inner London and broadly coincides with the boundaries of Camden Ward in the London Borough of Camden. In appearance it is typical of those residential areas undergoing gentrification. But a mile away a similar area known as Barnsbury in the Borough of Islington was one of the first areas to complete this process of working class displacement and by the end of the property boom in 1973 was completely "conquered".[2] However, in this particular neighbourhood, although the same forces were at work, the process of gentrification did not run its full course. Despite the improvement grants, the road closures and tree planting, the property speculators did not have quite the same success. Why this was so is the question this case study seeks to answer. The aim is to provide not a snapshot, exposing a particular housing situation, so much as an outline of events. In essence it is an illustration of the reality of housing as a factor in the daily reproduction of the social relations of capitalist society.

The neighbourhood in question does not exist in isolation but is a minute segment connected by a thousand threads to the rest of London, its places of work, magistrates' courts, hospitals, schools and centres of entertainment and relaxation. One in six of the population of Britain live in London. Yet despite the recent fall in its population it remains the one major area in the country where there are still more households than dwellings. Some of the country's worst housing conditions are to be found in its capital city. Scattered through the streets of London are tens of thousands of empty and decaying houses, dwellings without the full range of amenities, shared and overcrowded, and thousands of families and individuals are homeless. The worst conditions and most acute problems are concentrated in the declining private sector. Gentrification is its other face.

The population of London is falling. As a centre of employment it reached its peak in the early 1960s. At that time it was the country's biggest manufacturing centre with almost one million industrial jobs. One in five of the total labour force worked in the capital. Since then the population has fallen below 8 million and is expected to fall to 7 million by 1981.[3] This is the result of far-reaching changes in the location and organisation of industry and transport. Manufacture has been placed on a new technical basis, concentrated into new and expanded units of production, big capital has replaced small, and traditional engineering skills have become redundant. Transport has been reorganised and the role of the railways in conveying passengers and goods greatly cut back. In Inner London acres of marshalling yards lie empty and derelict.

The area of the study lies to the North West of three great railway terminals and their sidings: St. Pancras, Kings Cross and Euston. Until quite recently the neighbourhood was separated from two of the rail termini by various warehouses, light engineering workshops and wholesale produce markets. In the last decade or two all this has changed with the decline in the railways, the closure of the produce markets, and the rapid collapse of what was once a major centre of light engineering in and around Camden Town. In a comparatively short space of time a large number of skilled and semi-skilled manual jobs have gone. Figures for the Borough as a whole indicate the scale of the change: from the mid-1960s onwards 3,000 jobs have disappeared each year. By the end of the 70s unemployment rose to over 8 per cent. At the same time the Borough of Camden has declined in population at almost three times the rate for London as a whole. It fell from just under a quarter of a million in 1961 to an estimated 185,800 in 1976 and is still in decline.[4]

The immediate political context is important. The London Borough of Camden was formed in the middle of the 1960s as part of the re-organisation of London's local government. London County Council was replaced by the enlarged Greater London Council and the local boroughs re-grouped. Camden was formed out of the old boroughs of 65 years standing: Holborn, St. Pancras and Hampstead. The new local authority contained close to a quarter of a million people stretching from Covent Garden and Lincoln's Inn Fields in the South to Hampstead Cemetery, the Old Bull and Bush and Kenwood House in the North. Predominantly middle class Hampstead joined with largely working class St. Pancras and the more socially diverse and cosmopolitan Holborn to form the new unit of local government. In terms of party politics the new mix of local traditions and class strongholds—working class in central Holborn, Somers Town, Kentish Town and Kilburn, enclaves of intellectuals in Bloomsbury and even more strongly implanted in Hampstead, provided the basis for Camden's reputation as a progressive local authority, whichever of the two major parties formed the majority group in the Council.

The area

The neighbourhood is basically residential, consisting of some 2,500 dwellings inhabited by about 6,000 people. There were 4,052 people on the electoral register in 1978. Scattered throughout this pleasant-looking and seemingly quiet residential area are a number of small workshops: small-scale production, with little machinery being used, and in most cases employing only a few men and women. In reality they are survivals of what was once a common feature of the economy in London. There are workshops making clothes, a number of light metal trades are still in business, with some joinery and printing, and a dozen or so motor mechanics. Even so a number of small businesses have gone: the wholesale bakery and piemaker's, the blacksmith's and the piano and organ manufacturers. On the extremities of the area there is a small forge, a lorry park, a large car distributor and spares outlet and a big furniture warehouse belonging to one of the main department stores. There is a scattering of small builders' yards, one of them belonging to the local authority itself, and one large yard belonging to one of the major construction firms operating in North London and a well known employer of "Lump" labour.

The area is served by a number of small shops and has

three cafes and five pubs. In the middle of it stands the Irish Centre developed since the Second World War as a focus for the Irish in North London. It is run by priests who give advice and assistance, particularly for young people newly arrived from Ireland, and holds services and social events for the various Irish county associations and clubs. There is a Church of England Vicarage and Hall on the site of the original Church of St. Lukes, bombed during the last War. There is also a Spiritualist Church, the foundation stone of which was laid by the creator of Sherlock Holmes, Arthur Conan Doyle, in 1926. There are two day nurseries. One, held in the Church Hall, is expensive and largely serves middle class families from a catchment area much larger than the neighbourhood itself. The other is run by the local authority and caters for those having a priority need and draws from a large sweep of the borough. Finally, there is a local primary school, a Victorian building, which takes in the children of the area and the immediately surrounding streets.

The unity of the neighbourhood derives not simply from the clearly-defined boundaries of heavily-used roads, but also stems from its original layout and building in the middle years of the nineteenth century. The land once formed part of the Manor of Cantelowes and its freehold was in the possession of the Marquis of Camden. At the peak of Britain's imperial days the land was developed for middle class residence. Most of the housing is substantial in size, four storeys high, and wide stairways run up to the front door. The larger houses had stables and servants quarters to the rear and these form the two narrow mews which now house many of the workshops. A few houses still contain the old bell pulls that once summoned servants from the basement kitchen. The housing is built around two principal squares. The larger one of these contains a garden and a children's playground and supervised play centre. The other is a nursery with greenhouses and flowering shrubs and trees, hired out for displays, film and television sets and photographic work.

Developed in the early years of Victorian opulence, the greater part of the housing was enclosed behind brick walls, with the principal roads closed by imposing iron gates. A bell called the gate-keeper when admittance of a horse-drawn carriage or coal cart was necessary. It was thus separated from the notorious insanitary hovels of nearby Agar Town, demolished in 1866 because the development of St. Pancras station and its rail lines necessitated the enclosing with pipes of the Fleet Sewer. For half a century the estate was a preserve of the Victorian middle classes and only in the early decades of this century—and the removal of the large iron gates symbolised the change—did the servanted families give way more and more to workers and their families and members of the lower middle classes. Increasingly these large houses became multi-occupied, a family per floor and more. The stables gave way to workshops. Even before World War I the area was entering a new era which did not change significantly until the late 1960s.

The housing stock

St. Pancras Borough Council was a pioneer in the building of local authority dwellings. Even before World War I it constructed 207 purpose-built flats. In between the two Wars it built more than 1,000 such flats to rent. One of these projects in municipal housing included the construction of 95 flats, Camelot House, just to the north of the main square on the site of a former reservoir. It was completed just before the outbreak of the Second World War in 1939. Subsequent bombing of the area resulted in further major local authority construction to the south of the neighbourhood some years after the end of the War. Two sites were eventually cleared for redevelopment and two large estates, one of 188 and the other of 250 dwellings, built. So by the early 1960s, the local authority owned almost a fifth of the housing stock.

The 1961 Census indicates that two-thirds of the housing stock in the area was privately rented, with two out of three dwellings let as unfurnished. The mass of these dwellings were owned by small private landlords usually owning no more than a few houses, often in the same street. A local builder or trader or a family now retired and living outside of London were typical of the type of landlord. A number were resident landlords and perhaps owned a neighbouring house or two. Some of these landlords and their holdings have survived to this day and in many cases the same families and individuals are the tenants.

Some tenants had lived in the area for 30 or even 50 years, often in the same dwelling. In numerous instances these older tenants were tenants of the whole house and sublet floors to other tenants. At the end of the 1960s and early 1970s when property speculators began acquiring property in the neighbourhood, one of their first moves was to end these tenancy arrangements, thus clearing the way to raising rents as a lever to emptying properties for conversion and sale.

In 1961 only one in ten of the dwellings were owner-occupied. Again, some of these families had lived in the area for a long time. Not all the owner-occupiers were middle class—a number were working class families who had purchased their houses whilst sitting tenants in the 1950s. It was a settled neighbourhood with a complex and durable network of connections and contacts between individuals and families giving a degree of solidity and assurance to the immediate everyday life of the area.

The population of the neighbourhood in 1961 stood at 8,300 and probably three out of four lived in the private rented sector. The Census reveals that more than half the households in privately rented accommodation shared and in most cases lacked the exclusive use of at least one of the three basic amenities of hot water, fixed bath or inside toilet. Indeed, two of every hundred dwellings had outside privies. Overcrowding, where households occupy rooms at a rate in excess of 1.5 persons per room, was also prevalent, affecting some 1 in 6 of all private tenants, both furnished and unfurnished. There was a case of a whole family, including school-age children, living for some years, in a single room, albeit a spacious one.

In the 1960s this area of large houses was ripe for gentrification. Much of the housing was unmodernised, suffering from years of neglect and poor repair, multi-occupied, with families and individuals sharing inadequate facilities and often over-crowded. Changes in the ownership of the privately rented housing stock developed slowly during the 1960s. Property companies, generally on a small scale, began acquiring houses, while some landlords emptied their house or houses and sold with vacant possession. Census figures indicate that some fifty houses, representing between 100 and 150 dwellings, came into owner-occupation in the 1960s. But in 1971 over 60 per cent of all dwellings were still privately let, a proportion far above that existing throughout the country as a whole, yet typical of the residential areas of Inner London so sought after by the newly formed property companies and preyed on by the local estate agents.

The Conservative Government's proposed Housing Finance Bill in 1971, with the promise of all-round rent increases in both the private and public sectors and the final phasing out of controlled tenancies in low rateable properties, acted as a catalyst. The property boom was reaching its peak and the new Housing Finance Act of 1972, even before its passage, gave the green light to a mad scramble to acquire tenanted property for quick conversion. The new Act provided just the measure for shaking tenants out of their dwellings. It opened the way for providing basic amenities, and charging for them with increased rents, and having rents registered by rent officers and phased increases imposed. A study of rents in the area carried out in the early months of 1972 showed not only that registered rents were higher than unregistered rents, as was to be expected, but that where the basic amenities existed such rents on average were 50 per cent more. This was in April 1972. A flat in a converted house consisting of two rooms and its own kitchen, bathroom and toilet, on average had a registered rent, exclusive of rates, of £3.96, as opposed to £2.64 for a similar flat where the bathroom and toilet are shared. At the time a modern purpose-built local authority flat of the same size had an average rent of £2.65. A street survey of fifty dwellings conducted by the tenants association at this time revealed that 50% of private tenants, mostly unfurnished, paid £3 or less a week in rent.[5]

It was in these streets that the local estate agents and property companies increasingly became active in the early 70s. The street survey just referred to showed that half of the privately rented dwellings had come into the possession of property companies, the rest belonging to individual landlords, half of whom were resident. An illustration of what was happening is provided by the activities of a well-known property developer of the time, Mr. Timothy Gwyn Jones. Gwyn Jones headed a property empire involving 50 companies and owning hundreds of houses throughout North London. Through a company called Portland Management Limited he owned more than 50 houses in the London Borough of Camden, 9 of them in the immediate area of the main square at the centre of the neighbourhood. An investigation by the tenants' association brought to light his acquisition of property in the area and the consequence of his ownership. Five of the nine houses had been cleared of their tenants during 1971 and 1972 and were converted or in the process of being converted into flats for selling for owner-occupation. The other houses were generally in a poor state of repair, lacked a number of basic amenities and still had controlled tenants in occupation. This meant the purchase price of the property was low with the promise of a five-fold increase once emptied and converted.

It was precisely at this moment of rapidly-changing ownership in the housing stock of the area that the local authority, Labour-controlled, intervened with a plan to improve the whole environment of the neighbourhood. The impetus for the scheme came from existing residents, mostly well-to-do house owners already living in the area. They had formed a residents' group known as the Neighbourhood Association. It was very similar to the association formed in Barnsbury that had so successfully spearheaded the environmental improvements and rapid gentrification of that area. Very much a middle class grouping, it included among those active in it a number of architects, lawyers and accountants, as well as one or two with previous experience as Councillors. They proved a highly knowledgeable and capable pressure group. The primary aim of the Neighbourhood Association was to encourage interest in the local environment and pressure the Council into making improvements. It organised public meetings and social events and expressed an attitude of community spiritedness, again not unlike the Barnsbury group so much praised by planners at the end of the 1960s.

The activities of the Neighbourhood Association bore fruits with the introduction in 1970 on an experimental basis of the first of the environmental areas in Camden. In the first instance this involved the temporary closure of streets in order to check the cross flow of through traffic. The public were asked to participate in the experiment and an exhibition and meetings were held in the area. The tenants' association formed in January 1971 to fight the Conservative proposals for a new Housing Act objected to the scheme as irrelevant to the needs of tenants in the area. It was a protest largely ignored at the time as being out of place and divisive, as the environmental area would only affect the physical surroundings and movement of traffic, which, it was claimed, was clearly of benefit to all who lived there irrespective of whether they owned their dwelling, paid rent to a private landlord or were local authority tenants. The Chairman of the Neighbourhood Association at the time was a local resident deeply committed to the experiment as a project benefiting the whole community. During this period in his private capacity as an architect he filed planning applications for the conversion of no less than thirteen houses in the area and later became the architect in charge of the entire redevelopment of the Irish Centre.

Modifications were made to the closures and during 1971 the road barriers, and narrowings to stop heavy vehicles, became permanent. In the years immediately following the areas of the road closures were land-scaped, involving walled areas for shrubbery and raised paving. Trees were planted everywhere. Again protests that the tens of thousands of pounds involved could be better spent by the council repairing its own housing in the area were dismissed as irrelevant, as these things came under different departments of the Council. Eventually two of the more elaborate projects were abandoned for simpler ones, but this was due as much to newly imposed restrictions on the local authority's spending as to the protests of the tenants' association. In 1974 the Department of the Environment approved the designation of a large part of the neighbourhood a Conservation Area. This meant that the housing, its condition and improvement, was subject to approval by the local authority under the watchful eye of its Conservation Committee for the area which included representatives of the Neighbourhood Association. Ironically the protected area closely coincided with the original boundaries and iron gate-ways of Victorian times which were then meant to keep out the poor of the surrounding districts, only this time it was the three largest local authority estates comprising 537 dwellings that were effectively cut off by closures.

The environmental area was not the cause of the area's gentrification; rather it was a consequence of a process already underway. It undoubtedly helped push up property values in the area, which increased five-fold in the ten years since 1969. Also it helped push up rents and rates in the area. In combination with the peak of the property boom and the Housing Finance Act the private rented sector rapidly declined. Furnished tenants were fairly easily removed. The chairman of the newly-formed tenants' association appealed in October 1971 to the Rent Tribunal against the increase in his rent and was given the maximum protection then possible, six months, and invited to return again when the time was up. But the following year the family living above him in the same house were less successful. The *Camden Tenant* reported at the time:

"They appealed to the same rent tribunal against their rent being increased from £5 to £7 for two rooms. Their case was heard by the same three judges. The judges said the increase was reasonable . . . They also agreed with the landlord that the two-roomed flat was two separate one-room flats, in spite of the fact that the landlord had furnished one room as a bedroom with a double bed, and the other room as a living room with a kitchen not accessible from the bedroom . . . As a result of this decision a notice to quit against the husband is held in abeyance for six months but a notice to quit against the wife still stands. The wife could not attend the hearing because she was in hospital having a baby . . ."[15]

By the end of the year the family moved and the top half of the house was not relet. Within a year the tenants' chairman moved when offered a place outside the borough by a housing association. With only six months protection possible under the law and the owners anxious for vacant possession, the strain on the family was enormous and the chance of a proper flat and some security was accepted.

In the unfurnished sector, property companies overturned long-standing arrangements concerning payment of rents and rates and changed the tenancy arrangements in individual houses, in order to push up rents to the maximum possible, offering alternative accommodation to some tenants, and a few hundred pounds to others. It was often sufficient just to get one family out of the house in order to create a sense of the inevitable move to come amongst the remaining tenants. The tenants' association canvassed continually door by door with leaflets, arranging public meetings encouraging all with an interest in what was happening to the area to attend and join the fight to protect the interests of the tenants. This involved representing tenants at Rent Tribunals and in court hearings and making representations to the local authority. The Association surveyed the area pinpointing empty property—over 50 dwellings were empty by 1973—and listed all cases of landlord-tenant friction and harassment. Exposing the empty property, the conversions selling at "luxury" prices and the plight of tenants was the focus of activity. A number of actions were taken to highlight the problems: occupation of a show house, selling for £52,000, one Sunday afternoon when opened for viewing by prospective buyers, the take-over of two local estate agents offices in opposition to their part in the emptying and selling of property in the area, and the invasion of the offices of the Council's Director of Housing in protest against its inefficiency in dealing with local problems that were its responsibility.

In the end the area has not undergone the more or less comprehensive gentrification that has happened in nearby Barnsbury and to many other districts throughout London. Two factors account for this. The first is that the Council already owned a substantial amount of property in the area, and, secondly, the pressure brought to bear by the local tenants' association, by combining with the tradition of municipal socialism still alive in the Borough, resulted in the acquisition of a large number of houses by the local authority. Between December 1973 and the spring of 1975 the Council acquired 67 individual houses, the equivalent of some 200 or more dwellings.

A number of people active in the tenants' association remembered, and some had been involved in, the St. Pancras rent battles of ten years before and the radical Labour Council that preceded those battles. Organising tenants in the early 70s meant re-establishing links with a political experience vital to many working class men and women. It was not simply a question of an active local tenants' organisation successfully applying pressure on a local authority but much more a matter of bringing together those forces and traditions of municipal socialism embedded in the experience of thousands of working class people and activists in the Labour Party and amongst some of the Councillors themselves. These traditions of municipal socialism go back to the founding of the old St. Pancras Borough

Council at the beginning of the century and were embodied in the Labour Council elected in 1956. Its leader, John Lawrence, said after the election that the new Council would act as a Socialist one. On May Day they gave the Town Hall staff the day off and flew the Red Flag. One of the Councillors of the time, Charles Taylor, expressed the spirit animating the Labour group:

"We regarded housing and slum clearance as our first priority. But as the Tory Government were cutting back funds for such purposes, we decided to trim the ship. We considered the Civil Defence programme, to which the Borough had to contribute thousands of pounds, an absolute sham: what the hell was the use of stirrup pumps, sandbags and brown paper—the then official anti-glare protection—against the atomic bomb? Six to eight units of housing could be put in the Borough's Civil Defence headquarters alone. We refused to pay, preferring to put the money into housing for the people of St. Pancras. The Home Office sent in a Commissioner to adminster Civil Defence in the Borough.

"We made other savings. We went through the Mayor's diary and decided that there were hundreds of engagements of simply no consequence to the people of St. Pancras and that the Mayor's role should be strictly confined to chairing Council meetings, attending Old Age Pensioners' tea parties and going to children's Christmas parties. We also took away the mayoral car, saving hundreds of pounds. This upset the established order of things, created a real furore. But as Lawrence said: what was wrong with the Mayor going on the 68 bus?"[7]

The crucial issue was the 1957 Rent Act. The Council paid the increase for tenants living in derequisitioned property. This broke the rules governing local authority finances and 23 Councillors were surcharged by the District Auditor. They were disowned by the Labour Party nationally and in the summer of 1958 John Lawrence, Charles Taylor and twelve other Councillors were expelled from the Labour Party.

The local Labour Party was split in two by the expulsions and the Conservatives gained control of the Council. A means-tested rent scheme was introduced. This was resisted by the tenants who formed themselves into the United St. Pancras Tenants Association and organised a withholding of the rent increase. Some 8,000 tenants were involved in the struggle, which finally ended with massive police involvement in the eviction of two of the tenants' leaders, street battles with tenants and supporting building and railway workers, numerous arrests and a raising of class consciousness. "The rent struggle was a first exercise in community affairs."[8]

Many men and women—tenants and Labour Party activists—who had been involved in the St. Pancras rent struggles came to the fore again ten years later in opposition to the Tory Housing Finance Bill. Although St. Pancras was now part of the London Borough of Camden, sufficient local organisations existed—tenants' associations, trade union branches and local Labour Party and Communist Party branches—to quickly re-activate the combined experience of past struggles upon which to build a vigorous campaign against the proposed Act. Camden came to be one of the main centres of opposition both before and after the passing of the Act, with the Council delaying its implementation for six months.

The threads of this local political experience were drawn together in defence of workers and their families facing displacement from their homes. But in 1975 the Council's acquisition of housing in the area was abruptly stopped. The central Government, although Labour, acted to stop the wholesale municipalisation of private rented property. Camden acquired 2,000 homes in 1973 and 3,000 in 1974 and at that rate the end of private landlordism was in sight. To check further municipalisation on this scale the Government diverted funds into housing associations, and local authorities, such as Camden, were put in the position of having to support this stop-gap measure in home ownership. Public money from 1975 onwards went mainly into the acquisition by housing associations of tenanted and part-empty property coming on to the market. In Camden the borough was divided into areas and different housing associations were designated for each. In this particular neighbourhood the principal role was given to the newly-formed Community Housing Association.

By the end of the 1970s ownership of the housing stock had changed radically from what it had been less than a generation before. 1969 and 1975 were the peak years of the change. Since 1961 the privately rented sector has fallen from a little over two-thirds to less than a fifth (See Figure 2). The local authority owns well over a third, more than is owner-occupied, and one in twelve dwellings belong to housing associations.[9]

The coming battle

At the time of writing, in 1979, the neighbourhood is fairly settled in terms of the pattern of housing tenures. There are far fewer builders' skips and "For Sale" signs than a few years ago. The sheer size of the local authority share of the housing stock gives a degree of security and solidity to the working class of the area. In addition, most of the housing association tenants, at least half those in the private rented sector and probably 1% or even 2% of owner-occupiers are working class. Nevertheless, the middle class are in the ascendancy. Even the local branch of the Labour Party no longer meets in public premises but in the sitting room of one of the two houses belonging to its chairman. Unlike ten years ago, the middle class members now outnumber the working class men and women attending the Party's monthly meetings. Even the local cafe by the main Square, which for over twenty years served variations on egg, chips and beans, has changed its front, put cloths on the table and now serves lunches and evening dinners from a new frying pan to a quite different class of customer.

This shift in the balance of social classes is general to the Borough of Camden and London as a whole. As the population of London continues to fall so the class

Figure 2
Distribution of forms of tenure in the Camden Square neighbourhood
(Source: *Census figures and Camden Council records*)

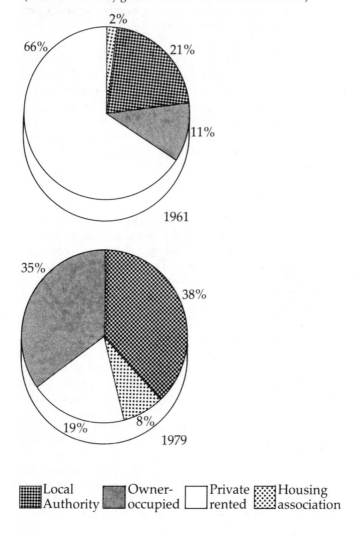

composition of the capital changes. Manual workers and their families are losing out in terms of both jobs and housing and are leaving London. At the same time there is a growth in the employment of women in non-manual working class jobs and a big expansion in the managerial and professional categories. The 1966 Census showed that the neighbourhood, compared to the Borough of Camden as a whole, had more semi- and unskilled manual workers and a smaller proportion of professional and managerial people:

	Percentage professional & managerial	*Percentage semi- and unskilled*
Camden	18	27
Neighbourhood	8	36

Recent figures point to a continuing rise in the numbers of professional and managerial people living in Inner London and a decline in all categories of manual workers. In Camden the proportion of professional and managerial has risen to 24%, while the number of manual workers generally has fallen and only 1 in 20 are now unskilled manual workers. The neighbourhood itself is losing population along with the Borough as a whole. Since 1961 it has fallen by a third in this particular Ward. Manual and non-manual workers have left while middle class people have moved in. Although there are no precise figures available, it is probable, given the pattern of tenure, that there are proportionally both more manual workers and professional and managerial people living in the neighbourhood than in the Borough of Camden as a whole. Politically the Ward remains a Labour stronghold.

For the majority of people living in the area, housing in its many facets remains an issue of immediate concern. On average rents in the area have tripled since the early 70s. Rents are no longer set at £3 and £4 per week in the case of two-bedroom flats but at £12 and £17 or more, depending on whether they are modernised and in council or private ownership. Then for those in the council sector there are the problems of getting necessary repairs done and the frustrations of dealing with the local authority bureaucracy. Converting the recently acquired property also creates acute problems for many tenants, and results in many unwillingly leaving the area to be rehoused in other council or housing association properties. Housing association tenants face the hardest situation. They have no security of tenure and no democratic rights when it comes to making demands on those who set themselves up in the management of these associations.

But for the neighbourhood as a whole the crucial issue and the key to present and future developments is the question of what happens to the remaining privately rented dwellings. These account for some 19 per cent of the housing stock. The owners are a mixture of old-time resident and absentee individual landlords and a handful of property companies that have survived a period of little movement in the property market. Problems persist in this sector. In flats that are modernised rents can be as high as £30 per week or more for two rooms, kitchen and bath. In other cases rents remain fairly low but the dwellings are unmodernised and the estate agents stay watchful and in contact with the owners. Some landlords are circumventing the law by offering people bed and breakfast instead of normal letting. One example will illustrate both the condition of much of the privately rented stock and the money to be made by this particular form of renting. The house is a four-storey terraced house, built in the middle of the 19th century. Ten rooms are let with a minimal amount of poor quality furniture in each. The house suffers from years of neglect and failure to do minor repairs when needed. Most rooms suffer from either rising or penetrating damp, ceilings are cracked, doors and windows ill-fitting and in a number of cases undersills and frames are rotting. Some of the rooms are partitioned and extremely small in size: two are only 11 feet by 8 feet. The one toilet for the whole house has no ventilation, a hole in the ceiling and water penetration. One basement room, 9 feet by 5 feet, and with no window of any sort, had a closing order put on it by the Council in 1978 and the old lady in her eighties who occupied it was rehoused. Only two of the tenants in the house are protected tenants and each has been attacked at different times by the landlord. One was punched and kicked, for which the landlord was fined, and the other was chased through the window of his room by the landlord brandishing a bread-knife. The other tenants, in order to avoid the protection offered by the rent acts, are given "breakfast" by the landlord. This consists of a box of six eggs, a loaf of bread, sugar and some tea bags, delivered each Saturday morning when the rent is collected. The landlord receives some £100 per week in rent from this house. The Council is presently considering, and likely to agree to, the tenants' association's demand that the house be compulsorily purchased by the local authority, although this is a slow process, usually taking one or two years or even longer to complete.

In its physical condition this house is typical of many of the houses still in the possession of private landlords, not only in this area but throughout the country. The aggressiveness of the landlord is less typical, although as such behaviour stems from the essentially antagonistic landlord-tenant relations it continually recurs. When property prices rise and the buying and selling of housing is on the increase and individuals and families are desperate for accommodation these sharp practices, such as "bed and breakfast", and the bullying increase. Millions of people still living in the privately rented sector face this burden of what others do to make their money. For the neighbourhood itself the outcome of these particular struggles and the success or otherwise in getting the local authority to acquire the property will have a decisive effect on the life and class strengths of those living there. A further wave of emptying and converting property for individual purchase will strike a blow at local working class organisations and political influence.

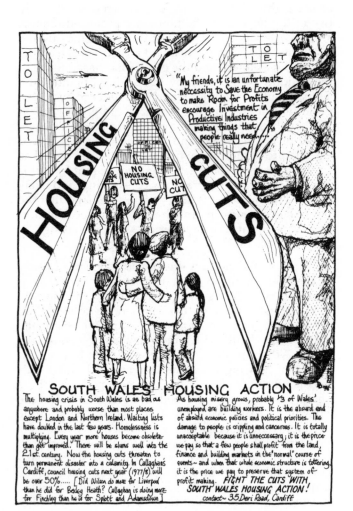

Chapter 6
Housing struggles

Past and present

Although the other side of the work-place is a place to live, when it comes to the development of working class organisation and politics in this country the struggles around housing appear quite insignificant in comparison to the part played by those waged in production. It is workers organised into trade unions who form the basis and the backbone of the labour movement. This is not in question. Yet struggles around housing are a vital part of working class experience and do play a part in the forming of working class political attitudes and outlook. What is needed, therefore, is an explanation of housing struggles in relation to the class struggle generally and an assessment of their political significance.

Under capitalism struggle is inherent in housing. Whatever the tenure, whether private, council or owner-occupation, the worker stands in an antagonistic relation to the landlord or mortgage company. In the latter case, the owner-occupier is generally isolated in his relation to the building society to which monthly payments are made, although even "home-buyers" occasionally organise themselves. In 1937 the Coney Hall District Residents' Association was formed in Kent to fight the building societies in the area. The action spread to other parts of the country and some 3,000 owner-occupiers went on mortgage strike because of the poor quality of their housing, which seemed likely to contravene local building regulations. As a consequence of the action some people were compensated, others lost out, and in 1939 an Act was passed protecting the building societies from having the validity of their mortgage deeds ever again questioned in such a way.[1] But such actions are exceptional, and generally owner-occupation is a tenure that enforces isolation more effectively than any other. In all tenures the struggle for most people, most of the time, is an individual one: getting the rent paid or a repair done and simply endeavouring to keep a roof

over one's head is an integral part of daily home life
for the mass of people. Homelessness always lurks in
the background, a threat that is never entirely dis-
pelled: an unexpected death, illness, loss of a job or
the break-up of a relationship may suddenly necessitate vacating the place in which one is living.

The work-place and the dwelling-place, the price of
labour and the price of housing in the form of wages
and rent or mortgage payment, are inseparably linked.
But unlike the work-place, when it comes to housing
the same enduring organisation and collective forms
of defence do not exist. Tenants' organisations, nationally and locally, have nothing like the permanence of
trade unions. Compared to the work-place the whole
character of housing struggles is precisely that of their
isolation and disparateness. Generally speaking, the
individualised struggles of people are only overcome
in very specific situations and for limited moments in
time, and organisation rarely outlasts the particular
battle, whether won or lost. Basically, people combine
together to defend themselves when they are threatened in their homes. Such attacks usually come in one
of two forms. First there is the direct threat of eviction
because of the impending demolition or conversion of
the dwelling or dwellings. This has happened again
and again throughout the history of working class
housing: the Somers Town Defence League in the
1860s and, a hundred years later in streets close by,
the Tolmers Village Association fought against wholesale slum clearance and the involuntary removal of
families and individuals from their homes. More com-
monly, combination comes about in order to fight rent
increases, the other major threat which strikes directly
at domestic financial arrangements. It is never simply
a matter of the rent going up, so much as the disrup-
tive impact such as an increase has on household
expenditure as a whole. Perhaps the best-remembered
rent strike is the one on the Clyde amongst munition
workers, which resulted in the state intervening to this
day in the regulation of rents and mortgage interest
rates. Again in 1938 there began a series of rent strikes
amongst decontrolled tenants in Stepney in the East

End of London. The housing was in the hands of private landlords and generally dilapidated. The strikes were against increases in rents and for the undertaking of basic repairs. Attempts were made to break the strike by carrying out summary evictions, but these were physically resisted, with the women of the East End leading the way. The landlords jointly issued a statement:

"The struggle in the East End is no longer a private matter between a particular landlord and his individual tenants. It is a struggle between mob law and the law and order of this country. The question arises whether an organised mob can defeat the orders of our law courts by physically preventing their enforcement. If the answer is in the affirmative, none of us in this country is safe with our possessions and rights."[2]

Despite their protests, the landlords were constrained to negotiate and eventually sign an agreement reducing the rents of all decontrolled tenants by varying amounts and promising to set aside specific sums of money for repairs. Again in 1968 tens of thousands of Greater London Council tenants organised themselves under the leadership of the United Tenants Action Committee to fight a large increase in rent to be phased over three years. In the end, after mass demonstrations, picketing and withholding of the increase, the Labour Government of the day intervened to stop further increases. The most widespread and generalised of all such tenants' struggles came in opposition to the Housing Finance Act in the early 1970s. It involved hundreds of thousands of tenants throughout the country in meetings, marches, pickets and partial and complete rent strikes. From 1972 through to early 1974, tenants in at least 80 local authority areas up and down the country were involved in the withholding of rent. Mostly this was a matter of not paying the increase, but in a few instances the strike was total. In the Tower Hill estate in Kirkby, Lancashire, some 500 tenants paid no rent and no rates for a whole year. Overall the fight against the Act played its part in the weakening of the Conservative Government and the return of Labour in 1974.[3]

Most struggles are defensive, fighting evictions or rent increases, and are attempts to preserve a given situation and level of rent. But occasionally there are actions that are offensive. This applies particularly to the periodic attacks made on empty dwellings in periods of widespread homelessness. Following World War II, ex-servicemen led the way in squatting empty property. After the Second World War the action was repeated on an even larger scale. In 1946 committees of ex-servicemen organised the placing of whole families into empty property. At first it was some of the large empty houses in southern seaside resorts such as Brighton and Southend-on-sea that were occupied. But the movement spread quickly throughout the country and disused officers' quarters on former military airfields were taken over. By October 1946 there were, according to the Government's own admission, "39,535 people squatting in 1,038 camps in England and Wales plus a further 4,000 squatters in Scotland".[4] The movement spread rapidly to the towns, and empty shops, disused schools and hotels, as well as houses, were squatted. In the middle of all this activity, "148 luxury flats in the Duchess of Bedford Buildings in Kensington were occupied and this seizure was followed by the occupation of flats and hotels in Marylebone, Holland Park, Campden Hill, Victoria, Regents Park, Bloomsbury and other key places".[5] This was in London, and Parliament was sitting. The Labour Government was forced to face the housing crisis. On the one hand, it condoned the arrest of a number of Communist Party members who were involved in the struggle but were by no means the main leaders or the instigators of the campaign. On the other hand, the Government legitimised the temporary occupation of many of the abandoned war-time camps and urged local authorities to arrange alternative accommodation for squatters, while the courts proceeded to grant eviction orders and in many cases houses and hotels were emptied with the help of the police.

Yet despite the successes of so many of these struggles in winning their demands or bringing about a change in the state's housing policy, no lasting organisation has resulted. The National Association of Tenants and Residents (NATR), formed in 1948, although surviving through to the 1970s never succeeded in either joining together the various tenants' associations existing throughout the country or in co-ordinating tenants' activities and their demands. It survived as long as it did because of the dedication and hard work of a small number of committed people who recognised the need for tenants to have an independent voice of their own when it came to issues affecting national housing policy. But neither in the days of the St. Pancras rent strike during 1961 nor with the much larger rent struggles of the GLC tenants in 1968 was the NATR able to exercise any influence or organise any support for those in struggle. The failure to provide any sort of national framework for tenants' activity was finally fully exposed during the campaign from 1972 to 1974 against the Conservative Housing Finance Act. In these years, tenants' activity and organisation throughout the country was stronger than on any previous occasion. In many of the traditional strongholds of municipal socialism, in South Wales, the Midlands and the North, and in parts of London, tenants combined with support from local Labour Party activists and others to fight the Act and the rent increases it introduced. In local authority housing the rise in rents highlighted the problem of the general condition of the housing: its faulty construction and poor state of repair. In the private sector rising rents led to pressure on tenants to vacate their homes so that property could be converted and sold with vacant possession. Rising house prices excluded most working class people from entering this tenure. Despite this drawing together of working class people in the different sectors, with their shared experience of poor housing at high cost, the campaign failed to consolidate nationally and was unable to put forward any programme of demands other than the general desire for the repeal of the Housing Finance Act. In this period of high and widespread activity all the NATR succeeded in doing was to organise two Parliamentary lobbies in the winter of 1972/3, hold a general meeting and produce two newsletters. It possessed neither the resources nor the political perspective for bringing together the various elements then in movement. Lobbying Parliament and local Labour Councils in itself was quite inadequate and inappropriate to the tasks at hand.

Now, in 1979, new efforts are being made to establish afresh a tenants' movement nationally, the National Tenants' Organisation (NTO). Actively supported by the Labour Party in the months before the general election, the initiators of the project produced a "Bill of Rights" for tenants, the Tenants' Charter. It paralleled proposals contained in the new Housing Bill, then being presented to Parliament but interrupted by the general election and now abandoned with the return of a Conservative Government. The effectiveness of the National Tenants' Organisation is unlikely to be very different from that of the old NATR that it replaces so long as tenants' associations and activity around housing remain so localised and disparate.

In relation to work

Why is it that in this vital area of working class life organisations of similar permanence to the trade unions do not exist? Why do tenants' associations appear so weak and ephemeral in comparison? It was argued in Chapter 1 that the capital/wage-labour relation is fundamental to the organisation of capitalist society and governs the social process of material production upon which life depends. This is the basis for speaking of the primacy of production and the economic character of the struggle between the capitalist and the working class. In production the conflict between the principal classes is immediate and ever-present, and results in the combination of workers and the formation of trade unions wherever there is production organised on a capitalist basis. In comparison, housing, where workers live in relation to their work, is a secondary, although clearly necessary, part of social existence.

But it is not simply a matter of correctly weighting these different elements constituting the material conditions of existence of the immediate producers. It is not simply that the social relations governing housing are subordinate to those governing the social process of production, but also that whereas the capital/wage-labour relation is direct and immediate in the factory, it is not so in housing. Finance capital, which dominates the housing stock, is mediated by the different agents of the various tenures: the local authorities, the small private landlord or property company, the building society or perhaps one's own employer (as with the banks and insurance companies). Together, the secondary position of housing and the indirect form of capital's rule weaken the necessity for combination in the defence of common interests. Consequently, tenants' associations remain but a shadow of their counterpart in production. Organisations on the basis of residence are both weaker and much more transient. They come and go and rarely achieve a level of combination, with everyone joining in whether actively or passively, as is achieved in many work situations. Even the most famous rent strikes of this century fall far short of achieving the solidarity characteristic of industrial disputes. The famous Tower Hill rent and rate strike in Kirkby against the Housing Finance Act did not involve everyone living on the estate in the year-long withholding. Workplaces put people together, shoulder to shoulder, creating the conditions for solidarity and collective action. Places of residence fragment people, each behind their own front door. This is true even on a local authority housing estate; it is even more so in streets where the ownership of the stock lies in varying hands, even if not those of the individual residents.

Yet despite the much greater fragmentation and individualisation of domestic life as opposed to work, the need for combination—however dulled—does exist, and from time to time and from place to place people do combine together and fight to defend or improve their housing situation. At the present time there are associations of council tenants, furnished and unfurnished private tenants in both permanent and short lets, lease-holders in blocks of flats, owner-occupiers in General Improvement Areas, and groups squatting unused dwellings. Together all these disparate groupings constitute the elements of the tenants' movement. In some local areas links exist between the various groupings, but regionally or nationally this is not the case. Historically it has proven very difficult, even on a local basis, to join together these various elements that make up the tenants' movement in embryo.

The spontaneous generation of these groupings is forever taking place. As forms of organisation they can be divided into two main types: those that are formed to fight a specific issue and those that are based on representing the general interests of a group of tenants. The first type may be a group of private tenants resisting a change in their tenancies, or an increase in rent or service charges, or perhaps a pending change in ownership and the threat of purchase by a company known for its speculation in property. This is also the nature of most organisations of tenants and/or owner-occupiers in General Improvement Areas. Squatters' organisations tend to be of the same type. The organisation exists to fight a particular issue, and its strength and survival depend on its ability to draw people into the campaign. These types of association come and go. Whether the battle is won or lost, the organisation rarely outlives the struggle. If it does survive, then it usually does so quite changed in its character and purpose.

The other type of tenants' association is the one formed to represent more generally the interests of a particular group of tenants. Initially these may be formed as the result of a particular problem, such as the need for major repairs or the installation of central heating. But as associations they survive on the basis of their ability to represent the more general and particular interests of tenants. This type of association is mostly to be found on local authority housing estates, although there are examples of similar general associations amongst private tenants. These associations also come and go, but their basis is of this general kind and they do tend to survive for much longer periods of time than the essentially single-issue associations.

It is quite probable that as many estates have tried and failed to organise themselves as have succeeded and that even more have never actually tried. But those that do succeed tend to be quite stable in their membership and leadership. Well-known local tenants' leaders tend to be such for a long time.

Against the social grain

Unlike workplace organising where the general interdependency of modern production and the mass character of the labour process is a basic condition for labour solidarity and unity, in housing organising goes against the social grain. The immediately given forms of family and personal life impose an isolation and fragmentation on social life which must be overcome in order to sustain any organisation. In this situation the existence of organisations of either of the two main types requires a commitment and effort on the part of the organisers. The single-issue organisations amongst residents in an improvement area or tenants in a block of flats that are up for sale or people occupying an otherwise empty property are brought together by the particular issue of improvement, change in ownership or threatened eviction. As a consequence these associations tend to be very energetic and lively, mobilising people to fight, and yet short-lived and rarely outlasting the particular battle, whether won or lost. They challenge authority and decisions that are being made and in this sense are highly political and usually appear so too—which is often at variance with the other type of association. The second type of associations also organise against the grain socially and require commitment and dedication, but their existence depends not on a single issue so much as the general situation of tenants, which usually means the numerous particular interests of those sharing a common residential area, such as a local authority housing estate. Indeed, many such local authority tenants' associations tend to be reluctant to fight critical issues such as rent increases and matters of general housing policy, as these may divide the members. Rather they rely on sponsoring social activities on the estate and taking up from time to time individual problems and common concerns regarding maintenance, caretaking and vandalism when pressed to do so. These associations tend to establish a working relationship with the local housing officers and local councillors. To a great degree their success depends on successful co-operation with the local estate office. In recent years a number of local authorities up and down the country have devised schemes by which these contacts between tenants' representatives and housing managers have become formalised. One of the most successful ways from management's point of view is the setting up of a committee structure which allows for regular meetings of tenants, officers and councillors and the discussion of immediate and pressing problems. Labour's 1979 Housing Bill intended extending this practice of tenants' participation generally throughout local authority housing. It is a principle likely to be pursued by the Conservative Government in the 1980s.

The fragile and transient character of tenants' organisations and the sporadic nature of housing struggles is rooted in the social relations of residential life that spontaneously divide and isolate people. Organising tenants is a matter of working against division amongst people. This explains both its weakness historically and its secondary importance in class politics. But these limitations, this weakness within the very basis of tenants' organising, is also its greatest strength in that it *does* necessitate going against the given order of things and overcoming the spontaneously imposed fragmentation and isolation of capitalist society. This is why the major housing struggles have nearly all involved an enormous release of energy and creativity on the part of those involved. It is not simply that people have created organisation where none existed and given leadership in situations with few parallels to draw upon; the very complexity of the housing situation has demanded ingenuity and the elaboration of direct forms of action, sometimes of enormous inventiveness.

This overturning of the given social forms of compliance characteristic of capitalist society happens again and again in all the major housing struggles. It is expressed most clearly in the central role played by women in most housing struggles, be they large or small. Phil Piratin describes how in Stepney before the Second World War he by chance stumbled on a problem troubling a number of residents in a block of flats: the lighting of the stairways by open gas-jet flares. He asked a woman if she could get some of her neighbours together. Within "ten minutes I was sitting around the table with half-a-dozen women drinking a cup of tea and listening to their stories about the gas lighting. How the wind blew it out, and the escaping gas could be smelt throughout the whole block. How the children would climb on each other's shoulders and light bits of paper from the flares, and all kinds of other very serious allegations about these conditions".[6] Anybody who has ever been involved in any tenants' organising will know that it begins with the women. They know the condition of the dwelling: the damp that brings mould to clothes in the bedroom, the draining board that is a health hazard, the faulty light switch, the window that cannot be opened and the door that can only be shut with shoulder and knee. Given the responsibilities for home life that capitalist social relations impose on women it is not surprising. But it is here in the dwelling, with the problems of its physical condition and monetary cost and its precariousness as a home, that from isolation women often come to act collectively.

On the Clyde in 1915, as pointed out in Chapter 2, women were at the centre of the struggles. Not only did they demonstrate and fill the court rooms, but they were the organisers. They made up the committees in the tenements and women were the block representatives. The Clyde struggle had its counterpart in other industrial towns at the time and again it was women in the forefront. Two thousand women marched to the Town Hall in Birkenhead behind the slogan:

"Father is fighting in Flanders,
We are fighting the landlords here."[7]

At the time of the Stepney rent struggle, just prior to the outbreak of World War Two, women were picketing the council estates in Birmingham against the City Council's rent increases. When the rent collectors appeared they were met by the women. "A whistle blew and hundreds of women came out of their houses with pots and pans, trumpets and rattles."[8] There has not been a housing struggle where women have not played a prominent part.

On the other hand, very often in the formal arrangements of tenants' associations, in officerships, and in formal representations to the local housing department or the landlord, men take their accustomed place. Here we confront that complex mass of threads that tie individuals to the established order of things and yet need severing if there is to be a development of class politics and a growth in consciousness of the need for fundamental change. Here we confront the fact that in all their weakness as a movement, tenants' organisations are collective forms vital to the growth in class experience and consciousness. They are not permanent and so central as the trade unions, but they do contain a shared class experience and are bearers of class consciousness. Historically, past and future, through these organisational forms and the struggles that erupt, women shape and share the consciousness of class.

Tenants' associations, like trade unions, are limited in what they can achieve. They are class organisations in a capitalist society. They give strength to the working class, and are part of the spontaneously created organisations that help make the class a social force, with a shared experience and separate identity. But they are not in themselves the vehicles, any more than the trade unions are, for overthrowing the rule of capital. At various times historically it has been widely believed by activists in the trade union movement that they could directly through the industrial struggle bring about the overthrow of capital, ignoring the existence of the capitalist state and its apparatus of violence. In a somewhat similar way, but with far less serious consequences for class politics, some activists involved in squatting empty property in the 1970s saw what they were doing as the direct appropriation of private property and a direct challenge to the capitalist order. The real need is to recognise the part that any tenants' organisations can play in the sharing, consolidation and transmission of class experience. This is as true for tenants' associations as it is for the trade unions, and will remain so even if there is little growth in the actual permanency of these organisations.

Although localised and disparate, such collective forms remain points of class experience vital for the survival of class identity in a capitalist society which forever is imposing its own forms and values upon people. This is why housing, however secondary it may be in terms of the overall struggle between classes within capitalism, remains a vital area of political experience. Although there is not the same immediate and direct conflict with capital as there is in industry, nevertheless there is the reality of the forms of capitalist social relations that effectively divide and weaken the working class. First and foremost there is the domestic situation: the position of the women in the family and the home. This fundamental social relation between men and women is affected by housing struggles and organisation—not necessarily dramatically and lastingly, but to the extent that women's experience can become part of the shared experience of the class. Clearly it represents an area that is badly undeveloped and yet of immense importance for the future making of working class politics.

Similarly, on the question of race, the consequences of internal splits within the working class are apparent. The problems of discrimination, fear and prejudice abound and especially where housing problems are at their worst. It is precisely here where the problems are most acute and are most divisive that the possibility for exposing the problems and working to overcome them is actually at its greatest. People do not have to like their neighbours in order to unite together, but a shared struggle helps more than anything else in overcoming individual fears, dislikes and differences. Again, tenants' organisation poses sharply the practical problems involved in working to overcome such divisions. For the uniting of all who are affected is a necessary aim for any housing struggle and yet extremely difficult to achieve. At the present time most tenants' associations are organisations with little immigrant participation of any kind, whether black or white, with the one exception of the Irish.

There is another dimension to the politics of housing, which involves helping to break down its isolation from the politics of the work-place. There are many aspects to this divide, as has been clearly demonstrated in recent years by the women's liberation movement. For the tenants movement the task involves not merely establishing connections with local trade union organisations, but getting across that housing is a matter of general political significance for the working class. At the present time such links are few and far between—and weak. Recent attempts in London and in the Midlands to establish joint action on the part of council tenants and workers in the direct labour departments of some local authorities have proved very difficult to translate into anything meaningful in practical and organisational terms. This is so despite the immediate material interests involved on the part of both the members of the direct labour force, threatened with redundancy under the public expenditure cuts by central government, and the growing problem faced by tenants of an already poor and deteriorating repair and maintenance service. Despite the shared concern in such work and the cuts to come, it is proving immensely difficult to build any campaign to defend and promote the joint interests. This underlines the long way there is to go in building any real links between the trade unions and other organisations and struggles outside the work-place. Nevertheless, such links represent the practical basis for any development of a genuine anti-capitalist politics.

Political independence

Tenants associations tend to have the appearance of dreadfully dull organisations. Like any organisation, they do have their routines of correspondence, minutes, collection of subscriptions and annual general meetings. But there is a deeper reason for this apparent dullness, in the strongly implanted tradition of keeping politics out of the business of the association. On the one hand, this means staying, at least formally, independent of party. This preservation of independence from the various political parties is an elementary condition for any such class organisation. Just as trade unions in principle are open to all, irrespective of party affiliation, so are tenants' associations. On the other hand, in the name of independence from party politics such class organisations are usually pretty effectively dominated by a politics: the politics of capitalist reform. This involves fighting for the immediate and particular interests of the members of the association as council or private tenants or as homeless people squatting. It is not unlike the trade unions with their concentration on the price of labour, wages. The fact that council housing or any other tenure, including owner-occupation, is enormously profitable to finance capital is rarely questioned, any more than is the continuance of wage-labour and its exploitation by capital. The proclaimed independence from politics in reality is very often little more than a spontaneous affirmation of a particular type of politics, the Social Democratic politics of the Labour Party.

The connection is not merely one of common ideology and acceptance of the basic capitalist order of things but also one of more immediate tangibility. The majority of tenants associations exist amongst council tenants. Most local authority housing is in the form of estates and these estates tend to coincide with the areas of Labour Party's political strength. Council housing is one of the major reforms accomplished by the Labour Party, comparable to the setting up of the National Health Service. So there is often a well-established link between local Labour Party organisation, council tenants and Labour Councillors. In many areas the individual working class members of the Labour Party are largely drawn from amongst council tenants. At election time the Party activists concentrate on "get-

ting out the vote" from the council estates. Many tenants' leaders are also members of the Labour Party.
These ideological and institutional connections are
interwoven into the tenants movement and help to
give it its strength as a factor influencing local Labour-
controlled councils and the overall attitude of the
Labour Party towards housing. At the same time this
connection excludes the formulation of more radical
ideas and demands with which to challenge the existing housing situation.

Any advance in the tenants movement, not in terms
of its numerical strength so much as in its conception
of the housing situation and the main demands
around which it organises, will necessitate a much
greater degree of autonomy from the Labour Party and
its politics than exists at present. It is not that the
political struggle can simply be by-passed—it cannot.
But if the politics of housing is ever to be posed in
terms of a real and lasting solution to the housing
question as an ever-present problem, then the politics
of accommodation to the capitalist order must themselves be challenged. If this challenge is to have any
historical significance, it must eventually find expression in a development of a politics and party organisation that goes beyond Social Democracy and poses
fundamental solutions to the real problems of capitalist
society. But this is a task that in itself lies outside as
well as inside tenants' organising and requires a separate, although related, development. All that basic
class organisations such as tenants associations and
trade unions can do is to play their part in reproducing
and helping to strengthen the identity and capacity of
the working class as a social force. This involves developing its autonomy from the capitalist politics of
reform. On the one hand, it requires struggling for
organisational forms that are capable of asserting the
immediate interests of people in specific class terms,
which means they should be as genuinely collective
and open as possible. On the other hand, there needs
to be some basic idea of the solution that is concretely
possible, historically, to the housing problem and that
can guide and inform such work. These two questions

are inseparably linked, but for purposes of exposition each will be treated on its own. It is not a matter of offering abstract answers to real problems faced in housing so much as pointing out the real possibilities for development in the tenants' movement which will help in eventually equipping the working class with the politics necessary for its own emancipation, and that of its allies.

Collective action

All the examples of major housing struggles mentioned at the beginning of the chapter were forms of class action independent of conventional party politics. Political activists of various party affiliations were involved in these struggles, but the unity of action and the demands that were made were independently formulated. The major rent strikes, fights against eviction and occupations of empty property were assertions of immediate material class interests. The web of party connections and party interests was subordinated to the demands of the struggle. The most recent and widespread of tenants' actions, the campaign against the Conservative Housing Finance Act in the early 1970s, fell short of such independent class action. Throughout the campaign and in most areas of activity there was an on-going struggle over the issue of whether to directly resist and make unworkable the implementation of the Act or to channel efforts into the established electoral process and the return of a Labour Government. On the one hand, this combination of positions and the forces involved explains the scale of the campaign, while on the other hand, it accounts for the outcome of Parliamentary compromise and retreat and the abandonment of rebels, whether Labour Councillors as in Clay Cross or striking tenants as in Kirkby and elsewhere. Actions that are independent of the electoral bargaining process are not necessarily revolutionary actions; they do not always bring into question the existence of the capitalist state, but they *are* autonomous in their assertion of class interest and power. It is not that they lack organisation and direction, that they are mere spontaneous explosions without leadership, but rather that they take a direction and produce a leadership which is independent of the capitalist political process.

Although for long periods it may lie dormant as an issue, the need for a real, as well as formal, independence of tenants' organisations is always there. It asserts itself as a practical matter again and again in local organising and activity. It is in periods of struggle that the possibility and need for genuinely independent collective forms of organisation arise. In the neighbourhood involved in the process of gentrification described in Chapter 5, it was during the period of most intense pressure on working class households that the tenants association was formed and was at its strongest and most innovative and expressive of local working class interests. The tenants association made public what was happening in the area. Isolated individual events affecting hundreds of people were brought out into the open and became issues of local attention and concern. Whatever the local Council did or failed to do and the activities of the local property speculators and estate agents became public knowledge. The association organised weekly open meetings in which the issues were debated and courses of action proposed and decided upon. These actions involved not only pressuring the local Labour-controlled Council but directly supporting tenants in their specific struggles with their landlords, exposing what was happening in the area by occupying a show house opened to prospective purchasers of some newly built luxury houses, attacking the incompetence of the local authorities by invading the offices of the Housing Department and organising protest occupations of the premises of the two principal estate agents locally. At the peak of the activity, groups of tenants canvassed each street in the neighbourhood with leaflets and loudspeaker, knocking on doors and conducting what sometimes became small impromptu street meetings. The tenants association created an open forum, a place for public debate of the immediate issues of concern to the area, and a means by which decisions could be taken and those responsible held accountable. It brought politics into the streets, creating an elementary form of democracy not so different in essence from the democracy of the public squares of Ancient Greece. Only a pinprick perhaps, but nevertheless it punctured the normal procedures and conventions of parliamentary politics.

Social ownership

The Social Democratic solution to the housing problem is for the state to provide for those in need. This development of the local authority tenure meets working class housing needs in a way that neither of the other main tenures can. Yet by presenting council housing as the socialist solution to the housing problem, the Labour Party has done a disservice to both the council tenure and to socialism. The state provision of housing takes place within the framework and dictates of capitalism. This means that council housing is indebted to the private interests of finance capital, is poorly built and maintained, and managed by a rigid and paternalistic local bureaucracy. Local authority housing meets working class needs more effectively than the other tenures, but does so in subordination to the interests of capital. Council housing should be seen for what it is: the only viable solution to the housing problem available under capitalism. This is not to imply that its quality and general standards cannot be improved—they can. But how far will depend ultimately on the balance of class forces and the ability to shift the balance of the division of the social product away from capital to the advantage of labour. The council tenure, then, does not represent a socialist solution to the housing problem in the sense of anticipating the sort of housing that will exist under the conditions of a developing socialist society. On the contrary, the social ownership of housing that will develop in a socialist society in its transition to a fully developed communism will be completely and utterly different.

Social ownership means that peoples' relations to the products of their labour and natural resources, and to each other, are no longer determined by their class position, but depend upon the relations governing their mutual co-operation in work and social life: property will no longer be private, belonging to a section of society, but social in character. The immediate producers will own and control, through the forms of their social co-operation, the social process of production. Similarly with housing, people, through the collective arrangements of their community and neighbourhood life, will have a real say in the type and quality of housing constructed and control its repair and upkeep. It will no longer be shoddily built for profit but will be produced and allocated in order to fulfil individual and social needs.

It will not be just a matter of sound physical structures that is at stake, but also the kind of space the dwellings and community facilities provide for the various activities of domestic life: child-care, housework, entertainment and relaxation. Under socialism these activities will progressively lose their narrow character at present imposed by private family life. This does not mean the abolition of an exclusive personal and home life, but rather overcoming its isolation and so strengthening the basis for individual participation in social life. In the past decade women have posed once again the question of their liberation from the narrow confines of domestic labour and stressed the social aspects of such work. They have demonstrated the possibilities for mutual support for those who suffer from domestic confinement, and the immense benefits for all arising from sharing child-care and other tasks to do with the home, such as the co-operative purchase of food. These experiments represent not so much the forms of the future as an expression of present needs unfulfilled by the existing order of social relations. In themselves these developments suggest that, far from being a precarious refuge from a hostile world, the home could become a point of entry into the immediate life of the community.

Clearly the social ownership of housing will involve an entirely different organisation of society to that which exists today. It will be based on common ownership, co-operation and the equality of freely developing individuals. It is essential to combat the conception of socialism that defines it as a little more and better managed and maintained council housing with its minimum of communal facilities. On the contrary, it will mean the end of council and all other housing tenures as we know them, for in reality they are all forms of capitalist ownership. It is not unlike the question of welfare, where socialism means not more meals-on-wheels, school dinners, social workers or play centres for school drop-outs, but the abolition of such welfare measures. Social relations will be totally transformed, allowing for the development of quite new forms of co-operation, domestic relations and forms of culture and individual expression. If this is beginning to sound like utopian dreaming, it is but a sober reminder of the grim realities of the inequalities and antagonisms, the isolation and anxiety, that forever are a part of capitalist social relations. Housing is not only affected in its provision by material inequalities, but is also the focus for many of the tensions generated in personal life by the general insecurity of a highly competitive society. It is women, in their traditional role as home-makers, who today suffer most from mental stress and depression.

None of the political parties that have shown any interest in housing struggles over the years make even the slightest attempt to elaborate a conception of the social ownership of housing and what it might mean in terms of housing provision and the transformation of the social relations governing domestic life. Both the Labour Party and the Communist Party give the solution to the housing problem as a further extension of state provision co-existing with the other tenures. According to the *British Road to Socialism* a socialist Government carrying through the revolutionary transformation of capitalist society will not touch the freehold of the owner-occupier.[9] At stake here is a misconception not simply of the major housing tenures and their relation to finance capital but also as to the very nature of the state and its involvement in the provision of housing. The state is not some autonomous apparatus subject to the will of the party in power, but is the state of capitalist society and exists in its historical elaboration to maintain the social and political conditions of capital's rule over the immediate producers. This is why a basic idea of what is meant by social ownership in relationship to housing is required, not because it lights up the imagination (although that is much needed), but for the break it involves with any notion of provision by the existing apparatus of the state. On the contrary, the existence of the capitalist state prevents any fundamental solution to the housing problem. So council housing, which is the only tenure under capitalism capable of meeting working class housing needs in any effective way, nevertheless will be abolished in the process of socialist transformation.

The struggle for working class organisations that are not immediately subordinated to capitalist politics, and the development, only sketched here, of the idea of the social ownership of housing are the basic issues at stake in the future growth of the tenants' movement. It is in this context that the demands for the nationalisation of land, the building industry and private financial institutions will need to be formulated. It is also the context for exposing present attempts to incorporate tenants' organisations into the activities of the state through mechanisms of tenants' participation in control, when effective ownership in a material sense still rests firmly in the hands of the capitalist state and the institutions of finance capital. In raising these points one is forced to face the present backwardness of any and all existing socialist politics in the sphere of housing.

Individuals, in their separate, private houses or flats experience only too directly the importance of good housing for the quality of life. But, given that housing is such a vital and sensitive aspect of the social relations of capitalist society, it needs to become a much more important focus of our political activity. If this does happen, it will be because women, who experience the importance of housing most directly, once again make it a matter for common struggle.

References

Introduction

1. *Housing Policy, A Consultative Document* 1977, Cmnd 6851, p. 10. For a critical discussion of the figures and the actual size of the surplus, see B. Crofton, 'Hard Core Mythology', *Roof*, March, 1979, 51–4.

2. *Up Against A Brickwall*, SCAT pamphlet, 4–7.

3. S. Alderson, *Housing*, 32.

4. P. Beirne, *Fair Rent and Legal Fiction*, 146.

5. F. Engels, *The Housing Question*, 41.

6. K. Marx, *Wage Labour and Capital*, 55–6.

Chapter 1   Capital and the housing stock

1. F. Engels, op. cit., 46.

2. E. Gauldie, *Cruel Habitations*, 189.

3. F. Engels, op. cit., 53.

4. A sales enticement of the time quoted in A. Briggs, *Victorian Cities*, 27.

5. From the introduction to E. Chadwick's *Inquiry into the Sanitary Condition of the Labouring Population of Great Britain* (edited by M. W. Flinn), 6.

6. F. Engels, *The Condition of the Working Class in England*, 81.

7. E. Gauldie, op. cit., 192. In March 1979 it was announced that Unilever are to sell the 900 houses of the village of Port Sunlight and so finally dispense with "tied" cottages. One suggestion is that the village could eventually become "a playground for the rich. A far cry from the original plan of providing homes for factory workers." *The Guardian*, March 15 1979.

8. P. Beirne, op. cit., 108.

9 For a brief discussion of tied cottages and farming see H. Newby, C. Bell, D. Rose & P. Saunders, *Property, Paternalism and Power*, 163–7.

10. S. Weir, 'Farm Workers' Rents', *Roof*, July 1977.

11. W. Harvey Cox, *Cities: The Public Dimension*, 19.

12. D. Massey & A. Catalano, *Capital and Land*, 79–86.

13. D. V. Donnison, *The Government of Housing*, 227.

14. *North Shields: Working Class Politics and Housing 1900–1977* (North Tyneside CDP), 10–11.

15. W. Harvey Cox, op. cit., 16.

16. A. S. Whol, 'The Housing of the Working Classes in London, 1815–1914' in *The History of Working Class Housing* edited by S.

D. Chapman, 18.

17. J. R. Kellett, *The Impact of the Railways on the Victorian Cities*, 294.

18. 'The Promised Land', *Camden Tenant*, No. 20, November 1974.

19. F. Engels, *The Housing Question*, 71.

20. "About 4¾ million houses were built in England and Wales between 1871 and 1918, of which 4¼ million to 4½ were still standing in 1975 . . .", *Housing Policy Review*, Technical Volume Part I, 4 (HMSO).

21. *North Shields: Working Class Politics and Housing 1900–1977* (North Tyneside CDP), 11.

22. *Housing Policy Review*, Technical Volume Part I, 5 (HMSO).

23. F. Engels, *The Housing Question*, 20–1.

24. F. Berry, *Housing: The Great British Failure*, 114.

25. S. Pollard, *The Development of the British Economy, 1914–1967*, quoted in A. Glyn & B. Sutcliffe, *British Capitalism, Workers and the Profits Squeeze*, 27.

26. D. Massey & A. Catalano, *Capital and Land*, 69.

27. ibid, 123.

28. ibid, 69–97.

29 N. Branson & M. Heinemann, *Britain in the Nineteen Thirties*, 205.

30. ibid, 206.

31. ibid, 200–222.

32. P. Ambrose & B. Colenut, *The Property Machine*, 41.

33. ibid, 41.

34. ibid, 28.

35. B. Dumbleton, *The Second Blitz* (pamphlet), 4.

36. *Housing Policy*, Technical Volume Part I, 74.

37. *Report of the Chief Registrar of Friendly Societies for 1969*, HMSO, 1970. Quoted in 'The Irrestible Rise of the Building Societies', *Roof* July 1976, 105.

38. ibid, 105.

39. M. Ball, 'Housing Policy and the House Building Industry', *Capital and Class* Spring 1978, 93.

Chapter 2   Family, home & state

1. E. Wilson, *Women and the Welfare State*, 115.

2. J. Foster, 'Nineteenth Century Towns—A Class Dimension', *Cities in Modern Britain* (eds. C. Lambert & D. Weir), 133.

3. A. Oakley, *Housewife*, 38.

4. K. Marx, *Capital*, Vol. I, 492.

5. ibid, 481.

6. A. Oakley, op. cit., 44.

7. Quoted in S. Alexander, 'Women's Work in Nineteenth Century London; a Study of the Years 1820–50', *The Rights and Wrongs of Women* (eds. J. Mitchell and A. Oakley), 406.

8. *Report from the Select Committee on the Health of Towns*, June 1840, quoted in J. Morley, *Death, Heaven and the Victorians*, 7.

9. E. Chadwick, *Inquiry into the Sanitary Conditions of the Labouring Population of Great Britain* (ed. M. W. Flinn), 8–10.

10. K. B. Smellie, *One Hundred Years of English Government*, 103–4.

11. *Housing Policy*, Technical Volume Part 1, 3.

12. E. Chadwick, op. cit. 194–5.

13. ibid, 205–6.

14. A. Oakley, op. cit., 54.

15. K. B. Smellie, op. cit., 104.

16. *Housing Policy*, Technical Volume Part I, 4.

17. A. Briggs, *Victorian Cities*, 226.

18. A. S. Whol, op. cit., 19.

19. ibid, 20.

20. M. Kaufman, *The Housing of the Working Classes and the Poor* pp. 91–92.

21. E. Wilson, op. cit, 110.

22. E. Gauldie, op. cit., 221.

23. J. Hilton, *The First Shop Stewards Movement*, 125–6.

24. D. Byrne & P. Beirne, 'Towards a Political Economy of Housing Rent', *Political Economy and the Housing Question*, 55.

25. F. Berry, op. cit., 34.

26. ibid, 40–1.

27. E. Wilson, *Women and the Welfare State*, Red Rag Pamphlet No. 2.

28. F. Berry, op. cit., 209.

29. D. J. Smith, *Racial Discrimination in Britain*, 293. For a detailed examination of the housing conditions of immigrants in the three main tenures private, council and owner-occupation—see 210–308.

30. F. Engels, *The Housing Question*, 42.

31. J. Lambert, C. Parris and B. Blackley, *Housing Policy and the State*, 36–64.

32. D. J. Smith, op. cit., pp. 260–1. For an informative discussion of procedures followed by local authorities in "fitting" tenants to dwellings see S. Demar 'A Note on Housing Allocation', *Housing and Class in Britain*, (Editors M. Edwards et al), 72–4.

33. T. Angotti, 'The Housing Question: Engels and After', *Monthly Review* Volume 29, Number 5, 43.

Chapter 3 The production of housing

1. T. Angotti, op. cit., 42.

2. F. Berry, op. cit., 94–5, and 232–7.

3. For a concise outline of the theoretical issues involved in establishing the place of housing in capitalist production see M. Ball, 'British Housing Policy and the House Building Industry', *Capital and Class*, Number 4.

4. These calculations are made from information provided in P. Beirne, *Fair Rent and Legal Fiction*, 188.

5. *Building with Direct Labour*, 34.

6. ibid, 33.

7. E. Gauldie, op. cit., 176.

8. M. Ball, op. cit., 83.

9. For the elaboration of such an argument see L. Needleman, *The Housing Question*.

10. *Building with Direct Labour*, 5.

11. J. Rogers, 'Anarchy in the UK Construction Industry', *Political Economy of Cities and Regions*, 17.

12. ibid, 19.

13. *Building with Direct Labour*, 44.

14. In the 1970s in the London Borough of Camden the Alexandra Road site built by Costains in the end cost almost five times its original costing of £5 million. *Camden Tenant*, Number 46.

15. M. Ball, op. cit., 82.

16. *Building with Direct Labour*, 41.

17. ibid, 27.

18. ibid, 43.

19. J. Rogers, op. cit., 20.

20. *Health and Safety Executive: Construction: Health and Safety 1976*, HMSO, 1978, quoted in *Building with Direct Labour*, 42.

21. F. Berry, op. cit., 259.

22. *Building with Direct Labour*, 14.

23. *Profits Against Housing*, 24–5.

24. *Building with Direct Labour*, 34.

25. *Camden Tenant*, Number 35.

26. *Building Design*, January 5, 1979.

27. ibid.

28. J. McQuillan and N. Finnis, 'Ways of seeing Dampness,' *Roof*, May 1979, pp. 85–89.

29. T. Angotti, op. cit., 42.

30. ibid, 42.

31. *Building with Direct Labour*, 99.

Chapter 4 Housing policy

1. P. Beirne, op. cit., 66.

2. ibid, 96.

3. *Houses—The Next Step*, HMSO, Command 8996, 1953.

4. *Homes For the Future*, Labour Party, 1956.

5. See D. V. Donnison, op. cit., 169–171.

6. P. Beirne, op. cit., 141.

7. *Signposts for the Sixties*, Labour Party Policy Statement, 1961.

8. See P. Beirne, op. cit., 132–8.

9. M. Ball, 'British Housing Policy and the House-Building Industry', *Capital and Class*, Number 4, Spring 1978, 94.

10. B. Kilroy, *Housing Finance—Organic Reform?*, pamphlet published by the Labour Economic Finance and Taxation Association, 22.

11. ibid, 18.

12. M. Ball, op. cit., 95.

13. M. Pawley, *Home Ownership*, 7.

14. ibid, 143.

15. P. Beirne, op. cit., 108.

16. ibid, 108.

17. V. Karn, 'Pity the Poor Home Owners', *Roof*, January 1979, 11.

18. D. J. Smith, op. cit., 239.

19. *The Government's Expenditure Plans 1979–80 to 1982–83*, Command 7439, 90.

20. Camden's *Financial Survey of Accounts*, 1971/2 and 1976/7.

21. ibid.

22. P. Beirne, op. cit., 106.

23. S. Schifferes, 'Living with the Cuts', *Roof*, March 1979, 49.

24. M. Pawley, op. cit., 7.

25. B. Kilroy, op. cit., 16.

26. 'The Irresistible Rise of the Building Societies', *Roof*, July 1976, 108.

27. S. Schifferes, op. cit., 48.

28. *Housing Policy: A Consultative Document*, Command 6851, 44.

29. ibid., 45.

30. ibid., 46.

31. ibid., 49.

32. B. Crofton, 'Hard Core Mythology', *Roof*, March 1979, 51–2.

33. *Roof,* March 1979, 41.

Chapter 5   Gentrification: a case study

1. *Camden Tenant,* No. 7.

2. A. Power, *A Battle Lost,* 1972. This pamphlet describes the process of Barnsbury's gentrification.

3. A. Kay, M. Mayo and M. Thompson, 'Inner London's Housing Crisis', *Community or Class Struggle,* (eds. J. Cowley, A. Kay, M. Mayo & M. Thompson), 132.

4. ibid, 132– 4.

5. The information is from a survey conducted by Camden Square Area Tenants' and Residents' Association.

6. *Camden Tenant,* No. 2, August 1971.

7. *Camden Tenant,* No. 19, September 1974.

8. ibid.

9. The exact number of local authority and housing association dwellings are known, but the numbers of owner-occupied and privately rented accommodation are based upon less precise information and are general approximations.

Chapter 6   Housing struggles

1. N. Branson and M. Heinemann, op. cit., 207–9.

2. ibid, 220.

3. L. Sklair, 'The Struggle Against the Housing Finance Act', *The Socialist Register 1975* (eds. R. Miliband and J. Saville), 250–292.

4. R. Bailey, *The Squatters,* 22.

5. ibid, 24.

6. P. Piratin, *Our Flag Stays Red,* 36.

7. B. Moorhouse et al, 'Rent Strikes—Direct Action and the Working Class', *The Socialist Register 1972* (eds. R. Miliband and J. Saville), 135.

8. Quoted in P. Corrigan and N. Ginsburg, Tenants' Struggle and Class Struggle', *Political Economy and the Housing Question.*

9. *The British Road to Socialism* (Draft) paragraph 1580.

Bibliography

ALDERSON, S., *Housing*, Penguin 1962.

ALEXANDER, S., Women's Work in Nineteenth Century London: A Study of the Years 1820–50. In *The Rights and Wrongs of Women* (Eds. J. MITCHELL & A. OAKLEY), Penguin, 1976.

AMBROSE, P. & COLENUT, B., *The Property Machine*, Penguin 1975.

ANGOTTI, T., The Housing Question: Engels and After, *Monthly Review*, Volume 29, Number 5, October 1977.

BAILEY, R., *The Squatters*, Penguin, 1973.

BALL, M., Owner-Occupation. In *Housing and Class in Britain*, Papers by the Political Economy of Housing Workshop, London, 1976.

BALL, M., Housing Policy and the House Building Industry. In *Capital and Class*, Bulletin of the Conference of Socialist Economists, Number 4, 1978.

BARKER, D. L. and ALLEN, S., *Dependence and Exploitation in Work and Marriage*, Longman 1972.

BEIRNE, P., *Fair Rent and Legal Fiction*, Macmillan, 1977.

BERRY, F., *Housing: The Great British Failure*, Charles Knight, 1974.

BODDY, M., Building Societies and Owner-Occupation. In *Housing and Class in Britain*, Papers by the Political Economy of Housing Workshop, London, 1976.

BRANSON, N. & HEINEMANN, M., *Britain in the Nineteen Thirties*, Panther, 1973.

BRIGGS, A., *Victorian Cities*, Penguin, 1968.

The British Road To Socialism, Draft Manifesto of the British Communist Party, 1977.

BRUEGEL, I., The Marxist Theory of Rent and the Contemporary City: A Critique of Harvey. In *Political Economy of the Housing Question*, Papers by the Political Economy of Housing Workshop, London, 1975.

Building With Direct Labour, Written by the Direct Labour Collective, London, 1978.

BYRNE, D. & BEIRNE, P., Towards a Political Economy of Rent. In *Political Economy and the Housing Question*, Papers by the Political Economy of Housing Workshop, London, 1975.

CAMDEN HISTORY REVIEW, Nos. 1 to 6, published by the Camden History Society, 1973–present.

CAMDEN TENANT, monthly tenants paper published by the Camden Federation of Tenants & Residents Associations, 30 Camden Road, London NW1.

CHADWICK, E., *Inquiry into the Sanitary Conditions of the Labouring Population of Great Britain* (Ed. FLINN, M. W.), Edinburgh University

Press, 1965.

CLARKE, S. & GINSBURG, N., The Political Economy of Housing. In *Political Economy and the Housing Question*, Paper by the Political Economy of Housing Workshop, London, 1975.

COCKBURN, C., *The Local State*, Pluto, 1977.

COLENUT, B., Behind the Property Lobby. In *Political Economy and the Housing Question*, Political Economy of Housing Workshop, London, 1975.

CORRIGAN, P. & GINSBURG, N., Tenants' Struggles and Class Struggle. In *Political Economy and the Housing Question*, Papers by the Political Economy of Housing Workshop, London, 1975.

CROFTON, B., Hard Core Mythology, *Roof*, magazine published by Shelter, March 1979.

DAMER, S., A Note on Housing Allocation, *Political Economy and the Housing Question*, Political Economy of Housing Workshop, London, 1975.

DONNISON, D. V., *The Government of Housing*, Penguin, 1967.

DUMBLETON, B., *The Second Blitz; The Demolition and Rebuilding of Town Centres in South Wales*, published by Dumbleton, 35 Deri Road, Cardiff, 1978.

EDEL, M., Marx's Theory of Rent: Urban Applications, *Housing and Class Britain*, Political Economy of Housing Workshop, London 1976.

ENGELS, F., *The Housing Question*, Progress, Moscow, 1970.

ENGELS, F. *The Condition of the Working Class in England*, Panther, 1969.

ENGELS, F., *The Origin of the Family, Private Property and the State*, Lawrence and Wishart, 1972.

FOSTER, J., Nineteenth Century Towns—A Class Dimension, *Cities in Modern Britain* (Editors LAMBERT, C. & WEIR, D.) Fontana, 1975.

GAVRON, H., *The Captive Wife*, Penguin, 1968.

GAULDIE, E., *Cruel Habitations*, Allen & Unwin, 1974.

GLYN, A. & SUTCLIFFE, *British Capitalism, Workers and the Profit Squeeze*, Penguin, 1972.

The Government's Expenditure Plans 1970–1980 to 1982–83, HMSO, Cmnd 7439, 1979.

HAMNETT, C., The Flat Break-up Market in London: a case-study of large-scale disinvestment, *Land, Property and Finance* (Ed. BODDY, M.) School for Advanced Urban Studies, University of Bristol, 1979.

HARVEY COX, W., *Cities: The Public Dimension*, Penguin, 1976.

HARVEY, D., *Social Justice and the City*, Arnold, 1973.

HINTON, J., *The First Shop Stewards' Movement*, Allen & Unwin, 1973.

HIRSCH, J., The State Apparatus and Social Reproduction : Elements of a Theory of the Bourgeois State, *State and Capital*, (Editors HOLLOWAY, J. & PICCIOTTO, S.), Arnold 1978.

HOBSBAWM, E. J., *Industry and Empire*, Penguin, 1969.

Homes For The Future, Labour Party Publication, 1956.

Housing Policy: A Consultative Document, including a technical volume in three parts, HMSO, Cmnd. 6851, 1977.

Houses: The Next Step, HMSO, Cmnd. 8996, 1953.

JONES, M. & HILL, R., The Political Economy of Housing Form, *Political Economy and the Housing Question*, Political Economy of Housing Workshop, London 1975.

KARN, V., Pity the Poor Home Owners, *Roof*, magazine published by Shelter, January, 1979.

KAUFMAN, M., *The Housing of the Working Classes*, EP Publishing Ltd, 1975.

KAY, A., MAYO, M. & THOMPSON, M., Inner London's Housing Crisis, *Community or Class Struggle* (Editors COWLEY, J., et al), Stage 1, 1977.

KELLET, J. R., *The Impact of the Railways on the Victorian Cities*, Routledge & Kegan Paul, 1969.

KILROY, B., *Housing Finance—Organic Reform*, pamphlet published by the Labour Economic Finance and Tax Association, 1979.

LAMBERT, J., PARIS, C. & BLACKABY, B., *Housing Policy and the State*, Macmillan, 1978.

LENIN, V. I., *Imperialism: the Highest Stage of Capitalism*, Progress Publishers, Moscow, 1964.

LUXEMBURG, R., *Reform or Revolution*, Pathfinder, New York, 1970.

MARX, K., *Wage Labour and Capital*, Moscow, 1956.

MARX, K., *Wages, Price and Profit*, Peking, 1970.

MARX, K., *Capital*, Volume 1, Moscow, 1954.

MARX, K., *Critique of the Gotha Programme*, Lawrence and Wishart, 1933.

MASSEY, D. & CATALANO, A., *Capital and Land*, Arnold, 1979.

McAVEY, K., City Life: Lessons of the First Five Years, *Radical America*, Volume 13, Number 1, January-February 1979.

McQUILLAN, J. & FINNIS, N., Ways of Seeing Dampness, *Roof*, magazine published by Shelter, May, 1979.

MILIBAND, R., *Parliamentary Socialism*, Merlin, 1961.

MITCHELL, J., *Woman's Estate*, Penguin, 1919, 71.

MOORHOUSE, B, WILSON, M. & CHAMBERLAIN, C., Rent Strikes—Direct Action and the Working Class, *The Socialist Register 1972*, (Editors MILIBAND, R. & SAVILLE, J.), Merlin 1972.

MORLEY, J., *Death, Heaven and the Victorians*, Studio Vista, 1971.

NEEDLEMAN, L., *The Economics of Housing*, Staples Press, 1965.

NEWBY, H, BELL, C, ROSE, D & SAUNDERS, P., *Property, Paternalism and Power*, Hutchinson, 1978.

North Shields: Working Class Politics and Housing 1900–1977, North Tyneside Community Development Project, 1978.

OAKLEY, A., *Housewife*, Penguin, 1976.

PIRATIN, P., *Our Flag Stays Red*, Lawrence & Wishart, 1978.

PAWLEY, M., *Home Ownership*, Architectural Press, 1979.

POWER, A., *A Battle Lost*, Friends Neighbourhood House Islington, London, 1972.

The Recurrent Crisis of London, Counter Information Services, London, 1974.

ROGERS, J., Anarchy in the UK Construction Industry *Political Economy of Cities and Regions*, Number 2, Architectural Association Planning School, London, 1978.

SCHIFFERES, S., Living With the Cuts, *Roof*, magazine published by Shelter, March, 1979.

Signposts for the Sixties, Labour Party Policy Statement, London, 1961.

SKLAIR, L., The Struggle Against the Housing Finance Act, *The Socialist Register 1975* (Editors MILIBAND, R & SAVILLE, J), London, 1975.

SMELLIE, K. B., *One Hundred Years of English Government*, Duckworth, 1950.

SMITH, D. J., *Racial Disadvantage in Britain*, Penguin, 1977.

Socialism and housing action, Socialist Housing Activists Workshop, Gateshead, 1979.

STEADMAN JONES, G., *Outcast London*, Oxford University Press, 1971.

Up Against A Brickwall, SCAT Publications, London, 1978.

WEIR, S., Farm Workers' Rents, *Roof*, magazine published by Shelter, July 1977.

WHOL, A. S., The Housing of the Working Classes in London, 1815–1914, in *The History of Working Class Housing* (Editor CHAPMAN, S. D.) Newton Abbot, 1971.

WILSON, E., *Women and the Welfare State*, Red Rag pamphlet Number 2, London, 1974.

WILSON, E., *Women and the Welfare State*, Tavistock, 1977.

ZARETSKY, E., *Capitalism, the Family and Personal Life*, Pluto, 1976.